A GREEN GUIDE TO COUNTRY SPORTS

A GREEN GUIDE TO COUNTRY SPORTS

Edited by
JNP WATSON

Foreword by
The Earl of Carnarvon

° THE °
SPORTSMAN'S
PRESS
LONDON

Published by the Sportsman's Press 1991

© The Sportsman's Press 1991

A catalogue record for this book
is available from the British Library

Photoset and printed in Great Britain by
Redwood Press Limited, Melksham, Wiltshire

CONTENTS

With illustrations by
Cecil Aldin, p. 15, 21, 22
Thomas Bewick, p. 37, 38, 41, 44, 51, 54, 81, 87
Lionel Edwards, p. 26, 29
Samuel Howitt, p. 95, 98
J. G. Millais, p. 25, 61, 66, 69
C. F. Tunnicliffe, p. 18, 35, 43, 45, 49, 53, 73, 102, 105, 107
etc

ACKNOWLEDGEMENTS

The publishers wish to thank the following for their help in finding illustrations: Edward H. Bryant of Vandeleur Antiquarian Books, London; Roy Heron, author of *The Sporting Art of Cecil Aldin*; Tom Quinn, author of *Angling in Art* and Tessa Reitman of Holland & Holland, Bruton Street, London.

They would also like to thank the British Field Sports Society for their help in compiling the list of Associations.

FOREWORD

by The Earl of Carnarvon, KCVO, KBE, DL

With more and more people visiting the countryside for their recreation and getting to know about farming whilst appreciating landscape and conservation of wildlife, one feature of the countryside is often missed out; that is recreation for those who live and work on the land.

A Green Guide to Country Sports provides the opportunity for those who wish, to learn about these different sports and the part that they each play in maintaining the countryside fabric as our heritage.

I must congratulate the authors, all expert in their particular fields, for providing us with a very enjoyable read for further education on the subject, and most important of all, for giving a better understanding of the part played by our countryside sports and their economic and environmental significance to the country as a whole.

CARNARVON

Chairman
Standing Conference on Countryside Sports

INTRODUCTION

Country Sports? Some people would include racing, golf, tennis, croquet, clay shooting, rally driving and hang-gliding in the definition. But, to the traditionalist, these are urban sports or merely games. The countryman thinks of rural sports in terms of those involving quarry animals: hunting, stalking, fishing, game shooting, wildfowling, coursing and falconry. And those are the subjects – most of them in one way or another, now controversial – with which this book is concerned.

Hunting was man's first profession and pursuit. In the beginning it was done to secure the protein – from fowl, fish and beast – on which he and his family were kept alive and well. After man the agriculturalist was firmly established, the sporting value of hunting and fishing was increasingly recognised. But man still loved that which he hunted, as he still does, and he treasured the unspoilt environment in which his quarries thrived. In Britain, in medieval times, the kings and the other great landowners jealously guarded their forests for the pleasure of their hunting and were thus conservationists. In the nineteenth century, foxhunters, owners of shooting estates and riparian-owning fisherman were to come, perhaps unwittingly, into the same bracket. It was not until the second half of the present century, however, that the country sportsman has become consciously conservationist.

We would not expect our book to find favour with the official 'greens,' that is to say those who belong to the British Green Party. For that matter our contributors (who might, if pressed, describe themselves as 'country greens') are unlikely to exhibit much sympathy for many of the principles of the political greens. Just listen to this rhetoric from the Kemp and Wall *Green Manifesto for the 1990s*, a document that has been rapturously acclaimed by the 'political' greens:

> 'Greens would end all bloodsports ... What is gentle about killing millions of pheasants, specifically bred, by blasting them out of the sky with a shotgun? What is gentle about deer stalking, angling or any other so-called sport that involves the murder of animals? The shooting gentry claim to be conservationists, but study shows this claim to be false. Grouse shooting – incidentally, a favourite pastime of Prince Charles and other Royals – means that heather moorland is burned every year to create the right conditions for grouse to breed. The burning exposes soil to erosion

and causes the pollution of our water systems. To add to this, far from ending their days on the dining table, millions of game birds are burned or buried because there is little demand for lead-infested birds . . . A Green government would ban fox hunting, hare coursing and similar abominations.'*

In Britain's town-orientated society those views, or a modification of them, are not limited to animal rights activists, left-wing intellectuals or militant vegetarians, but have a considerably broader base of support than they commanded in our fathers' day. Yet, although the chapters that follow here have little to do with green politics or liberal green thinking, we believe that they have much more practical and cogent messages for wildlife conservation than many of those propounded by the Green campaigners – such, for instance, as those of them who, in passing their verdicts on our country sports, show an extraordinary lack of understanding of Nature.

This book is aimed not so much at those who are already dyed-in-the-wool sportsmen, or on the other hand rabid 'antis', but more at those who are open minded enough to listen at least to argument based upon deep and long experience in the countryside. 'What is gentle about stalking?' ask the authors of the Green Manifesto. Well, we can only recommend you to read Richard Prior's chapter and see how 'gentle' life would not be for the deer without stalking! 'What is gentle about angling?' they ask. As Sandy Mitchell and Crawford Little point out it is the responsible fishermen, more than anyone else, who show real concern for the conservation of our rivers and lakes, who condemn pollution, poaching and callous treatment of fish.

'What is gentle about killing millions of pheasants?' Kemp and Wall want to know. For that matter what is gentle about killing millions of chickens and turkeys from poultry farms? But turn to Colin Laurie McKelvie and learn what good is done for our wildlife in general by responsible game shooting; and to the chapter on wildfowling by Arthur Cadman to learn how the 'fowlers are true to their pledge to 'put back as much as they take out'. The statement by Kemp and Wall on grouse shooting, too, is one of crass stupidity. If it were not for the conservation of our heather moors, the grouse would quickly decline; and, as for shooting them, that is considerably more humane than letting them die of starvation or disease within three years of hatching, which would otherwise be their lot. Anyhow, if grouse shooting ended, most of the moors would likely be turned over to sheep grazing or forestry, to point the way to the demise of the grouse. And, contrary to what those two green politicians say, heather burning does not cause pollution in any meaningful sense.

* Green Manifesto for the 1990s, by Penny Kemp and Derek Wall (Penguin, 1990), page 124.

Hunting the red deer with hounds in the West Country is perhaps the most controversial of our field sports – on account of the size, beauty and nobility of the quarry. Yet it is, by paradox, one of the most essential, in terms of the conservation of the creature concerned, and certainly the most natural method of culling. The subject, as we indicate, simply requires a closer examination than most non-hunting critics are prepared to give it. Foxhunting, too, receives much flak. The principal question we pose there is 'would the welfare of the fox be more or less favourable without hunting?' We know that he would be worse off. The Kemp and Wall document also describes hare coursing as an 'abomination', and we hope that Charles Blanning's powerful piece will help to redress the balance on that score. The *Green Manifesto* would doubtless include hawking under what they call 'similar abominations', and here Diana Durman-Walters gives us a refreshing concept of the wonderful conservationist work done for raptors by falconers. But for their devotion several bird-of-prey species would now be on the verge of extinction.

On the other hand we do not say with Voltaire that 'all is for the best in the best of possible worlds.' We question whether in foxhunting, for example, the acts of earthstopping, digging and bolting should – despite the need to reduce the fox population – continue, except where absolutely essential, in an age which demands greater humaneness in all dealings with animals. And certainly we do not think that digging should be a part of the sport as such. Arthur Cadman roundly condemns 'marsh cowboys', while Colin Laurie McKelvie despises game-shots who do not practise their skills; who do not take the trouble to retrieve and dispatch wounded birds as quickly as possible; and shoot organisers who ignore the ecological requirements of wildlife conservation.

Sandy Mitchell, supreme among today's young sportsmen-conservationists, takes a long hard look at the suffering that fishermen may cause their quarries and at the justice, or otherwise, of certain tackle. He frowns upon the release of non-native species, and upon 'banks mown like lawns to ease the fisherman's access and casting'. Because the green and humane aspects of fishing have always received a lower profile than that in other branches of country sports, we have given rather more space to them in this book.

Great Britain boasts as rich a country sports tradition as any other nation in the world, and a name, too, for responsible sportsmanship that must be second to none. Sportsmen everywhere are rightly proud of that national reputation. We hope that our readers, having absorbed all that is written here, will close this book with the impression that (although there is still much abuse of privilege by that small *selfish* element who carry guns and rifles and rods, who ride to hounds, fly hawks and run long dogs) it would be a tragedy for rural Britain if any of the sports were to be abolished on the whim of Parliament. If that were to happen, in any branch of our field sports, the umbrella organisations, who spell out the desired codes of conduct, would fold up; it would then be the outlaws who would triumph. (Certainly the law would do little to stop them.) We hope, too, that the wealth of information contained in these chapters will help convince the doubters of the considerable contribution that country sportsmen are making all the time to the landscape and its habitats.

Finally, although we may at times hold different views from the British Field Sports Society on the conduct of some of the activities discussed here we give that organisation our unequivocal support. The Society forms a splendid brotherhood and does monumental work in protecting the interests of country sportsmen, all of whom should belong to it.

J.N.P.W

HUNTING

J. N. P. Watson

J. N. P. Watson, the editor of this book, was educated at Eton and RMA Sandhurst. A former cavalry officer and commander of parachute troops, he has also been an all-round country sportsman since boyhood. He was field sports editor of *Country Life* from 1969 to 1987. The number of packs of hounds with which he has ridden (or run) in his capacity as that magazine's hunting correspondent, has earned him a place in the *Guinness Book of Records*. He is also a knowledgeable naturalist; and, in 1982, he was awarded a Travelling Fellowship by the Churchill Trust in recognition of his writings on animal welfare. He is the author of sixteen books, including seven relating to country sports, and editor of four other books.

HUNTING THE FOX

The fox exists throughout Britain – it exists in very large numbers, even in suburban areas – wherever there is adequate cover for the purpose of breeding and raising its families. As a predator it is either shot, trapped, poisoned, gassed or hunted with hounds. Foxhunting is carried out from November to March inclusive, preceded by cubhunting after the harvest. The humane factor in the sport has been so widely and so fiercely argued during the past half century, and with increasing tempo and impetus, too, that the subject became polarised long ago, with neither those in favour, nor those against, budging an inch in their adopted stances. At worse the foxhunter shrugs and says, arrogantly, that 'of course the sport must continue as it has always done, because it holds an integral place in British tradition and thousands of people enjoy the recreation so the moral question is neither here nor there. If ignorant "townies" don't like it that's their affair.' At worse, too, the abolitionist says 'foxhunting must be made illegal because the fox when hunted experiences the same sort of terror as I, the "anti", would feel in the same situation, which makes it outrageously cruel ... Also the "so-called sport" has to be abolished because it is indulged in by rich and privileged countrymen who show little courtesy for other people let alone compassion for animals.'

The appraisal that follows will attempt to cross-examine several firmly held opinions on both sides of the foxhunting fence; to take a fair and balanced account of whether the circumstances of chasing the fox to its death is justified in principle; to see to what extent we might condone any suffering that may be inflicted on a fox in the course of the hunt by comparing that with the suffering that may be involved in other forms of death to which foxes regularly succumb; of whether the general welfare of the fox would improve or deteriorate if foxhunting were to be banned by law; and of whether the sport is really healthy for the countryside.

Some of the animal-welfare societies would have us believe that the fox population finds its own reasonable balance season by season. But that is immediately disproved by the fact that farmers, gamekeepers and poultry-men everywhere find it necessary to destroy a volume of foxes that goes a long way into six figures annually. Those societies try to impress upon us, too, that foxes only take lambs that are already dead or too sickly to live more than another day or two anyway. Well, let them tell that to the sheep farmers of the Scottish Highlands and the West country, of Wales and the Welsh borders and of the northern counties of England, places where some farmers will be out all night banging dustbin lids or with a gun across their knees during lambing, to keep the predators at bay! The welfarists assert, too, that poultry enclosures are so impenetrable, given tough chain-link wire, as to deter even the boldest and wiliest of foxes. Why is it then that there are reports every day in every county, of hen-runs, duck compounds and turkey farms invaded, not with the loss of one or two birds, but of dozens at a time? It must also be remembered, that vulnerable free-range poultry farms have become much more widespread in recent years.

How does the fox, for the most part, die? His number one enemy is surely the motorist whose deadly wheels kill off by far the greatest proportion. Then, as stated, there is the gamekeeper – or certainly most of his profession – who, fearing for the security of his nesting birds and release pens, disposes of several thousand more. The sheep and chicken, turkey and duck farmers come next in the precedence of vulpicides. And, after them, the pelt-trapper accounts for a proportion, though mercifully (for his snares are usually ineptly set and he is inclined not to visit them regularly) he is a less common species than he was in the 1970s and '80s, the price once commanded by fox fur being severely diminished. Many thousands of foxes succumb to dis-ease, mange being the worst culprit here; others to starvation. Very few indeed reach the age their creator vouchsafed for them (eleven to twelve years). It is reckoned that the conventional foxhunts put an end to an average of rather less than two per cent of all that die per annum.

Which method of control inflicts the least suffering? Certainly not the trap or snare, which all too often results in slow strangulation, laceration, or the wrenching off of a foot, or – when, as so often happens, the trapper only returns to his snares after a long period – death by starvation on the spot. Nor the cage trap, the solution to fox control so often advocated by animal-welfare societies. For nothing is guaranteed to inflict greater terror and stress on a wild mammal, of the size and character of a fox, than to find itself imprisoned in the space of a wire cage, then to be faced by a man intent on killing it. (And the trapper, also, as I say, frequently forgets his trap.) Nor gassing, with its drawn-out suffocation (not to mention its impact on other wildlife in the vicinity). Nor the slow and violent agony of poison, which is anyhow illegal. Nor the shotgun, which as often as not results in gangrenous wounds rather than instantaneous death (partly because of the frequent inaccuracy of the men with guns and partly because they all too often shoot out of range, 15–20 yards being the absolute maximum distance that a fox should be taken on with a shotgun). But death from the hound pack is instantaneous – that is if the fox does not get away unscathed.

Returning to the subject of shooting foxes let us now see what lessons may be drawn from the activities of the gun clubs, those associations of farmers, shepherds, foresters and their friends who, in the sheep-farming districts of Wales, the Welsh borders, the Highlands of Scotland and parts of the West Country – where the huge tracts of conifer plantation form close fox strongholds – shoot them to protect their lambs, and for sport. Having sent their hounds into the evergreen woods to rustle up the foxes, the club members – perhaps as many as sixty or seventy men armed with shotguns – positioned on the perimeters, shoot the predators as they break covert.

As an example of how such activity affects a conventional hunt take the experience of the United, whose country, extending some thirty-five miles by thirty, lies in south-west Shropshire and part of Montgomeryshire, with kennels close to the centre at Bishop's Castle. The United share that domain with three gun clubs, two of which kennel substantial packs of hounds, the third being trencher fed. (It is laid down by the Masters of Foxhounds Association that no hounds from hunts registered with them shall be allowed to go to the gun clubs, but, willy-nilly, many do so.) It is estimated that, of the 700 foxes a year or so that die by deliberate human device in the United country, well over eighty per cent are destroyed by those three gun clubs. A great many more foxes are maimed by them for, as the United hierarchy report, their runs frequently finish with the death of an animal that has been moving on three legs, or is otherwise wounded, owing to gunshot wounds. (It would be more humane to use an effective small calibre rifle against foxes.) The pattern of that suffering is repeated more or less throughout Wales and the Welsh borders wherever there are forestry plantations.

But, so far as the conventional foxhunts are concerned, the menace of the gun clubs continues far beyond that. The farmers, whose main concern is the destruction of the lamb-predatory foxes, give precedence to the clubs to whom, *force majeure*, the hunts must defer when fixing their meets. And those privileged clubs go just about everywhere they please; private owners of woodland refuse them admission at their peril.

How, you may ask, are they financed? Well, as a start they are subsidised by the Forestry Commission, who, having created such formidable foxholding citadels, feel they owe a debt to the sheep farmers. So what an irony it would be if the relatively humane practice of conventional foxhunting were to be abolished by ill-informed politicians, on the grounds of cruelty, while the government-subsidised gun clubs, who really do inflict great suffering, were allowed to continue their pursuits as now. (But then that is the sort of wrong-headed decision-making affecting our wildlife that is inclined to be made in Parliament.)

Then, too, as 'green' sportsmen, we should address ourselves to the ethics of certain practices at the fox's earth, or lair, in traditional hunting. We refer to earthstopping and the digging out and bolting of foxes. Earthstopping is done to prevent the hunted fox finding his familiar refuges. Foxes are bolted with terriers either when the situation is such that it may be difficult to find above ground, or – when a fox has gone to ground – to give hounds another chance to catch him. Foxes are dug out of their earths during a hunt, either to be disposed of with a humane killer, or to be put on the move again for the benefit of a further hunt. Foxes are also dug out and shot because the landowners, etc., concerned request it; sometimes purely to give 'a taste of blood' to hounds that have not killed for some time; and, by some hunts, to entertain the members of the hunt supporters' clubs, those foot followers who regularly subscribe handsome sums of money or presents to the kennels, who enjoy 'a good dig' and who are seen to converge at an earth with relish when the terrier men are called up. (Incidentally, nearly all equestrian followers find digging both distasteful and tedious: distasteful because they regard it as being unnecessarily callous, it does not accord with their concept of fair sport; and tedious because it often means waiting about, cold and bored.)

Anyhow to what extent is all this interference with the fox's lair really justified in 'green' terms? Well, in many countries hounds would simply have no chance at all in catching up with their quarry unless there was some

earthstopping (which includes the blocking of entrances to stacks of straw bales). But, of course, the entrances must be unblocked once the 'stops' have served their purpose. And any earthstopper who contravenes the ethics of that role should never be permitted to have a hand in it again. If the hunts are drawing over, say, shooting estates or poultry farms they will often be obliged, by the landowner concerned, to account for foxes that find refuge in earths. Having said that, however, we would add that, as a policy, foxes that go to ground should be 'given best'. And, if there has to be a dig, we say that it should never be regarded as a part of the sport, and that no one should be allowed near the earth (or whatever) except the terrier men and those assisting them in the operation. Digging, bolting and earthstopping, albeit often necessary, comprise the ugly face of foxhunting.

By far the most tiresome mammalian pest, so far as lowland districts are concerned, is the rabbit, which has been returning in ever greater numbers since the 1980s. And, for that, farmers should in our opinion, welcome a healthy quota of foxes on their acres. Before our ancestors began messing up the ecology the wolf pack and the lynx were the fox's natural enemies; now only man fills that niche. Therefore let the hound packs be the successors of those long extinct predatory beasts. But let that pursuit be on just terms. Foxhounds should by and large either catch their quarry in the open or not at all. That way it is very often the sick, injured and old foxes that are taken.

There is another reason why digging is to be avoided if possible. Any Tom, Dick or Harry may dig foxes from their earths, provided they have permission from the landowner or farmer. Such activity takes little or no account of the code of the Masters of Foxhounds Association, whereby no human may so much as touch a live fox, and whereby pregnant vixens and litters of unweaned cubs are protected. Worse still, the legality of it inadvertently gives cover to the men who dig for, and otherwise persecute, the protected badger. If such criminals are caught in the act they can say it is fox, not badger, they are after; and, in attempting to substantiate that claim, they will often bring a dead fox to the badger sett on which they are at work.

To sum up on the humane issue, the fox is a potential pest and there are too many foxes in Britain. For the most part they die before their time (long before their allotted span) and they nearly all die relatively unpleasant deaths. To hunt foxes to their death with packs of hounds cannot be said to be the most effective way to cull those predators, nor, as we have seen, can it be claimed that the pursuit has any great impact on the fox population. But those who condemn the whole principle of hunting simply do not understand Nature. Hunting is the most natural – and, if conducted fairly, the least cruel – method of reducing the number. And the sport brings in its train a great many other benefits.

With regard to the mounted followers it has been described as being so exciting as to be like 'war, without its guilt, and with only twenty-five per cent of the danger'. A gross analogy? Perhaps. But the horsemen and women who indulge in the pursuit would not do so unless there was that risk that brings such excitement. There is too the inestimable thrill of seeing hounds race, close packed, on a good scent, of hearing their wonderful cry, of seeing them check, reclaim the line and run on again. There is the element of uncertainty – will the next draw fulfil its usual promise? Which way will the fox lead the pack, which way from this spinney or that gorse? Will the scent strengthen in the afternoon? And so on for four to six hours. Then there is the joy of a winter's day in the countryside; and there is the companionship, the social side of the sport, the chat as they trot from meet to draw, at covertside and hacking home. There is, too, the close interest that so many subscribers take in their hounds, and the breeding of their pack. (None of these pleasures exist, by comparison, in the brief cut-and-dried pursuit of draghunting, except in the smallest degree.)

Let us take note of the vast numbers of people from every walk of life who derive pleasure from the sport. There are over 200 packs registered with the Masters of Foxhounds Association. It has been conservatively estimated that some 50,000 men, women and children ride with them, and that a further 400,000 follow by foot, car or bicycle. For most it is their principal recreation, for which they sacrifice much; for many it is more than a sport, it is a way of life. The primeval thrill of the chase, the passion his and her remote ancestors knew, is in the heart of every genuine foxhunter. For them it is a most stimulating diversion.

As a by-product, it also provides employment for a great many people, not only at the kennels and stables, but at the saddlers, the veterinary surgeries, the studs, the blacksmiths, the animal-feed merchants and many others besides. For two centuries the breeding of hunters has formed a vital base for the bloodstock industry, and, more recently, for the production of showjumpers and eventers. That wonderfully successful organisation, the Pony Club, owes its launching, its framework and its fundamental character to the hunts, while, over and over again, the hunting-field has proved the most beneficial training-ground for the young equestrian. Nor must we forget the bright traditional pageantry that the hunting cavalcades bring to the British countryside, a much loved feature of our national heritage.

What has all this to do with the 'green', or conservationist, issue? Well, we mention these golden characteristics and bonuses in response to those who tell us that the pleasure which it gives to all those thousands of people scarcely justifies the small impact it has on the fox population, nor the damage inflicted on the farmland by the horses, not to mention the disturbance of the wildlife. To those who try to argue that the activity affords little positive benefit to the countryside we point to all those numerous coverts owned by hunts throughout Britain, coverts which provide rich habitats for a great variety of wildlife, and which would have been razed to make way for

pasture or arable many years ago if it were not for the continuation of foxhunting.

Wherever the sport flourishes in Britain landowners and farmers plant and maintain wild places or conserve places that were always wild, scrublands, gorse coverts, hedgerows, heathlands, spinneys or boglands by the hundred, as habitat for foxes – and thus for a myriad of other animal and plant life. On the other side of the coin it has to be stated that farmland has become so sensitive and the farming industry so fragile that it behoves the foxhunter, more than ever, to respect the land over which he and she rides – to keep to the headlands, not to gallop over very wet pasture, to close gates, to replace the wire they have cut and to mend the hedges and fences they have broken. It behoves them, too, to show greater courtesy than ever to the non-hunting public, whether road-users or people walking their dogs on public footpaths, whether villagers with pets or men working on the land.

But foxhunting is threatened with abolition by our politicians. So let us pose this question for them: 'Would the future of that predator be happier or more miserable if hunting was to be banned by law?' And let us answer it. We believe that the conventional foxhunters, those going about their business under the strict auspices of the Masters of Foxhounds Association, have the true interest of the fox at heart. The genuine foxhunter, lover of horse and hound, is – or should be – a full-hearted animal-lover in the general sense. And he looks upon the death of a fox, other than in the course of the chase, as a sacrilege; he discourages, and speaks out against, other forms of vulpicide.

He is determined on the one hand to control the fox and on the other to preserve it. He is, by paradox, the fox's first friend (much more his friend than the passive 'nature lover'). If foxhunting were to be banned by law that mammal would be more than ever at the mercy of shepherds, poultrymen, farmers and gamekeepers with their shotguns; of pelt-trappers with their snares; of poachers with their lurchers; and of foxbaiters with their terriers. We believe foxhunting to be at once a most worthy and beneficial recreation and the most humane (albeit perhaps the least effective) method of destroying surplus numbers of this handsome predator.

HUNTING THE RED DEER (West Country)

The only appreciable surviving herds of wild red deer in England have their home on Exmoor and the Quantocks, in West Somerset and a part of Devon, a total area of something over three hundred square miles, in which three packs of hounds are kenneled to hunt them – the Devon and Somerset, the Tiverton and the Quantock. Towards the end of 1990 the National Trust organised a referendum of its membership to ascertain how much support existed for deerhunting and foxhunting on Trust land. In both cases only a little over six per cent of the membership troubled to vote. Of that tiny minority a high proportion were either members also of, on the one hand, the British Field Sports Society or, on the other, of the League against Cruel Sports, both of which had naturally encouraged their members to join the Trust and take part in the ballot. The vote went in favour of continuing to have foxhunting on Trust land, but – by a narrow majority – to ban deer-hunting. The turnout being such a derisory figure – from a National Trust membership of some two million – the organisation's Council, for their part, decided not to act upon the vote. However, the main point of interest is that more members showed themselves to be against deerhunting than against foxhunting, which indicates that the larger and more noble an animal is the more closely people will identify with it, the more passionately anthropo-morphic their feelings will be, without consideration for the whole context in which those animals live and die and the problems they pose for the humans alongside whom they have their being. For, in fact, the case for the hunting of the wild red deer, our largest mammal is, as we shall see, rather easier to argue than that of the hunting of the fox.

Those who follow the staghounds take great pride in their quarry and in their knowledge of its life history and characteristics, which are as follows. To begin with the deer's life cycle, the calves are born in June. They are not always well guarded by their dams and many are taken by foxes. The young stag, in his second year, shows no more than knobs where the full horn will eventually appear, the size of his antlers growing annually until, by about the age of eight, he should carry his adult quota of twelve points. (There are records of 17–20 points.) The antlers are deciduous, that is to say that the stag sheds them every spring and immediately starts growing new horn in the form of highly sensitive blood vessels covered with a protective grey substance known as velvet. During August when the horn is fully grown, the blood supply dries up, the horn solidifies and an intense irritation sets in. The stag will then seek a suitable tree, usually a sapling (referred to as a 'fraying stock'), on which to rub off the maddening velvet. The exposed white horn gradually weathers to coppery brown, leaving only the tips of the points white.

The rut, or mating season, lasts, roughly, from mid-October to mid-November. It is then that the master stags appropriate their harems, roaring, or 'belling', to drive away rivals. At rutting time, too, the stags wallow in mud and peat, perhaps refreshing themselves, perhaps also rendering themselves more awe-inspiring. Deer may live fifteen to twenty years, their longevity being determined by how long they can escape disease and how long they keep their teeth. Once they lose those they will die by starvation, more likely than not in mid-winter. The seven-month gestation period implies that hinds will be at the climax of their pregnancy in May–June, thereafter rearing their young. Thus hinds are hunted from mid-November through February and stags between August and October. There is also spring staghunting (March–April), for which animals of three years old, or thereabouts, are the quarry. The close season is from the start of May to mid-August.

Now we turn to the *raisons d'être* of hunting. As a start the deer must be quite severely culled for their own sake. If left freely to their own breeding dynamics they would outstrip their food supplies and therefore die by the hundreds of starvation. Secondly, they cause extensive damage. They invade the farmlands and eat the corn; they tear up root crops, turnips and potatoes, or nibble at one root and pass to another. Worse still they use the cornfields as daytime dormitories, rolling in them, or basking. And they eat the young shoots of trees. In the Highlands of Scotland these problems are conveniently dealt with by high fencing, the woodland and farmland there lying apart from the moorland, the home of Scotland's red deer; whereas, in the West Country, woodland, farmland and moorland are inextricably mixed, which makes such partition impracticable. In Scotland the deer are culled by professional marksmen and by stalkers. But, again, this is not nearly so easy in the more heavily wooded and trappy conditions of Exmoor and the Quantocks. There, too, the practice poses a danger to other humans. It has always been the case that, in contrast to the situation in the open Highlands, a much higher proportion of shot deer in the West Country have got away wounded. By law a deer becomes the property of anyone on whose land it strays at any given moment, and they frequently become the target – not to be killed, but to be injured – by farmers with shotguns in Somerset and Devon. And there is a good price to be fetched for venison.

In the early nineteenth century when the pack of hounds hunting Exmoor was sold to a German purchaser, shooting became rife, and, by the time the next pack was established, in 1855, the herd was reduced to no more than fifty animals, of which many were found, by the new hunt, to be wounded by gunshot. By the 1890s the three packs that are hunting Somerset and Devot today were already in operation. Deer hunting soon became a firm tradition, while farmers and their families, devoted to their respective packs and to their regular days out with them, were, as they remain, quite prepared to put up with a measure of damage in return for their sport.

Four centuries and more ago in Britain it was not necessary for humans to cull deer, which were then hunted and killed by wolves, their natural predators, working in packs. The wolves chased the deer until it chose a spot – a stream, a hillock or a patch of thick cover perhaps – at which to stand at bay, to use its antlers in the case of stag or its sharply pointed, cloven feet in the case of a hind. The wolves, having surrounded it would close in for the kill. Nothing could be more appropriate than that the hound pack should replace the wolf pack. That which accords with Nature cannot be unkind. The only difference in the picture is that the hounds do not touch their quarry; when the deer stands at bay – or is surrounded swimming in a river – it is shot with a humane killer by the huntsman. It either dies on the spot or it escapes, unscathed. The venison goes to the landowner or tenant over whose land the deer was hunted; the offal to the hounds.

Hunting is carried out by the Masters of the Devon and Somerset, the Quantock and the Tiverton staghounds to a strict code of conduct. The

tactics of the hunt ensure that a suitable beast is hunted according to the time of year. The harbourer is the expert who, the day prior to the meet, sets out to the area concerned to select a 'warrantable' deer, which in autumn means an old stag. Then he returns early next morning to ascertain its movement. At the meet he informs the Master where the selected animal is lying. While the main body of the pack is kept in reserve for the time being, four or five couple, the 'tufters', are taken out to rouse the deer concerned and separate it from the herd. When it is clear away and running the rest of the pack are unboxed and laid on its line, and so the full hunt commences.

New followers often express surprise at the nonchalance of the hunted deer. Indeed it nearly always seems quite confident that it will elude the pack, confident, too, in the power of its deadly antlers or its feet to win the fight when standing at bay. Notwithstanding the dramatic press photographs we are sometimes shown and the disgust often expressed by weekend visitors, who do not understand the true nature of deer and deerhunting, everything about the pursuit speaks of humaneness. Of common sense, too: the maxim 'no hunting, no deer' is a proven truism. And everything about it speaks of good conservation. For the hunting folk,

who form a close and jealous brotherhood, cherish the land of the deer, which contains some of the most breathtakingly beautiful scenery in Britain. Those who ride (or otherwise travel) with the staghounds are the ones who will do most to fight for the integrity of Exmoor and the Quantocks and their outlying corners which form the habitats for the last of our English wild red deer.

HUNTING THE FALLOW BUCK (New Forest)

The New Forest owes its existence to the chase. Those lovely woodlands were first established as a Royal hunting park in the eleventh century by King Canute and were taken over as such by William the Conqueror, whose son William Rufus was killed while deer hunting in the Forest. The Forest's fallow deer have been hunted there from that day to this. But there was one very black period: 1851–54. The Deer Removal Act was passed in 1851 to gratify the Forest Commoners who erroneously believed that their cattle and ponies would enjoy twice as much grazing if the deer were destroyed. The unfortunate beasts were then trapped, shot, netted and hunted down with bloodhounds until there were very few left, and Gerald Lascelles, who was to be the Forest's Deputy Surveyor and its greatest ecologist, wrote that 'the palmy days of the beautiful old Forest came to an end'. Nor did the domestic stock grow fatter, for holly and other rough pasturage, to which the deer were not impartial, invaded the grassy swards everywhere. Ironically the cattle and ponies had less to eat than ever. Although it proved impossible to eliminate the deer the fact that they were decimated made conventional, properly conducted hunting a lot easier. The Deer Removal Act being rescinded in 1854, another of the Forest's great naturalists, Henry Buckworth Powell, founded what was to be the forerunner of the present pack. The next Master was Francis Lovell, one more devoted conservationist, and then Lascelles himself (who also acted as huntsman), a man whose life was largely dedicated to the study of the Forest's wildlife and its preservation.

Since the early years of this century the Forest has supported three packs of hounds, foxhounds, buckhounds and beagles. Although other species of deer now inhabit the Forest it is only the fallow that is hunted and only the male, the buck. The fallow's life cycle is much like that already described for the red deer. Hunting is an official element of the culling programme. While the Forestry Commission, which is the monitor of the deer, takes its toll with the rifle, its keepers, of whom there are about a dozen, act as harbourers to the New Forest Buckhounds. Nowadays – in contrast to red deer hunting in the West Country – a 'warrantable', or huntable, buck has come to mean a somewhat inferior specimen, because the Forestry Commission likes to save the biggest and best to maintain the quality of the stock. Nor does it allow the hunt to pursue the rare menil, or relatively black, bucks. But 'warrantable' very often means a wounded animal because poaching is rife, despite the vigilance of the keepers; and other deer are sometimes maimed in the course of legitimate shooting. The hunt frequently disposes of lame animals.

The principles of hunting are otherwise much the same as in the West Country. A few couple of hounds, the 'tufters', are taken from the meet to rouse the buck selected by the harbourer, to ease it away from other deer. Once it has been separated and got fairly on the move the remainder of the pack is brought up. During the delay the buck may have as much as three-quarters of an hour start. If hounds do come up with their buck he stands at bay or lies in thick cover. In either case he is put down by a member of the hunt staff with a humane killer. The season runs through from September to April, except for the period of the rut.

There are no greater lovers of the New Forest and its fauna than those who follow the fortunes of the Buckhounds.

HUNTING THE HARE

The hare, unlike its cousin the rabbit, lives above ground and is unsociable, a lone creature. Its home is its form, a mere scrape or slight depression in the ground. It depends for its survival mostly upon its exceptionally acute hearing, its facility for prone, motionless concealment and its tremendously fast stride. Its strong scent is its main handicap, but it is wily in tricking its pursuers – by deliberately passing through herds of cattle or flocks of sheep, crossing and recrossing fences, walls or streams, or pushing another hare off its form and lying there itself. Its main enemies are man, fox, stoat, weasel and dog – man because of his relentless, hyperactive farming methods; fox, stoat and weasel because of their facility for nosing out very young leverets; and dogs, chiefly in the form of lurchers used by poachers. A hare must use all its wits all of the time if it is to enjoy even a brief life in the bustle of the modern countryside.

Farmers like to see plenty of hares shot, on account of the damage they do to crops, particularly vegetable crops (ten hares are said to eat as much in a day as a sheep). Many people who are invited to hare shoots, however, and who hear, for the first time, the cries of a wounded hare, vow they will never risk repeating that harrowing experience. Conversely, nearly everyone who starts to follow harehounds – harriers (followed mounted), beagles and bassets (followed on foot) – will never witness the wounding of a hare, and will be more than likely to make a habit of the diversion for the rest of their lives. Actually, if they are beaglers, it may be a long time before they ever

witness the death of a hare, not only from the difficulty of keeping up with hounds, but also because a kill is quite rare in that activity. 'Anti-blood sports' people have been seen to demonstrate at meets of harehounds in recent years as much as at those of foxhounds and deerhounds. Few people in this world have possessed a deeper knowledge either of hare's natural history or of hare hunting than Bill Lovell Hewitt. Let him speak on the subject of the ethics of the sport:

'It is in crediting animals with the imagination and knowledge of humans that the uninformed go so far astray. They assume that animals suffer from fear of what may happen, when they, in fact, have no mental power to imagine anything not actually experienced. Knowing nothing about death, or being ill or being crippled, the animal suffers from none of the fears that bedevil the human race . . .

'The animal, having no power of imagination, fears only those things it knows from actual experience can cause it pain. The hare has no fear, as we understand fear, of being pursued by hounds. It has never been hurt by them, and it has never been caught by them, nor by any of its pursuers. The natural instinct of every wild creature is to run, fly or hide from a strange thing . . . That is all that actuates the hare while she is being hunted. The idea that she is in terror of being torn to pieces by the hounds is simply nonsense. It is as great nonsense as the idea that those who hunt her are actuated by sadism.'

Harehunting has a much older tradition than foxhunting. After Hugo Meynell and others rendered foxhunting so popular after the mid-eighteenth century, by speeding it up, the older generation of countrymen mourned the pushing of the harrier into second place. This verse from Wilfred Scawen Blunt's poem, *The Old Squire*, reflected the sentiment:

> *I like the hunting of the hare;*
> *New sports I hold in scorn,*
> *I like to be as my fathers were*
> *In the days ere I was born.*

There are twenty packs of harriers in mainland Britain. Being heavier and longer in the leg, and thus faster, than the foot packs, modern harriers (foxhound-beagle cross) catch considerably more hares. But the foot packs enjoy longer hunts. There are over eighty beagle packs and some dozen of bassets, involving over 10,000 regular supporters. Beagling takes place between October and March, so that the hare is left (anyhow by conventional harehunters) to breed in peace, and the crops to grow undisturbed. Harehunting is selective in that it is usually the older or diseased hares that are caught, while the young, fit hares invariably go free.

There is nothing quite like following hounds for sensing a close involvement with Nature, for being caught up in the rhythm of the predatory wild; and, of all branches of hunting, there is probably none that promotes this involvement more robustly than beagling or following basset hounds. For the foot followers, not being concerned with handling horses and having few of the equestrians' problems in crossing the countryside, may absorb themselves entirely in the career of the pack – and the huntsman and his whippers-in – and in the observation of hounds pitting their strength and their wits against a wild animal on Nature's terms. It is from that experience, week in week out through the season, that hunting men and women appreciate how wonderful the countryside is and how precious its wildlife habitats. This is what prompts them to be the champions of all wild life and the guardians of what is left of our unspoiled landscapes.

HUNTING THE MINK

The two most damaging mammalian pests in Britain are the rabbit and the mink; the rabbit (notwithstanding myxomatosis) because of its voracious appetite for the farmers' crops; the mink because of its appetite for the farmers' poultry and duck, and, much worse still, its appetite for a large variety of our wild fauna, from robins and kingfishers to voles, from moorhens to crayfish.

Mink is the name given to certain members of the family *mustelidae*, to which the badger, stoat, weasel, marten and polecat all belong. Regarding the mink now at large in Britain its colour, in its wild state, is usually dark brown; its size is larger than that of a stoat, smaller than a polecat. It is aquatic in habit, feeding on fish as well as birds and small mammals. Mink can climb and burrow, as well as run and swim. A pair of them will work their way along the banks of a stream, killing and eating just about anything that moves, and when their young can fend for themselves the whole family will move onto fresh hunting-grounds. If there is one mammal that has done more than any other to reduce the populations of our songbirds, waterfowl and harmless rodents, it is the rapacious mink. It will attack new-born lambs and even ewes, whose udders it will gnaw at if it gets a chance. There have been reports, too, of it going for domestic pets. In short it is a principal curse of the countryside.

It is not, of course, indigenous to Britain, but is the descendant of escapees from fur farms and only became a serious nuisance as late as the 1970s. If – as say a poultry farmer – you ask the RSPCA how to deal with it they will make one suggestion only – cage traps. But a few traps set close to chicken farms or ornamental duck compounds, or whatever, will have very little impact on the mink menace in the wild at large. How easy are they to catch? Not at all easy, for although they are inquisitive, they are not unsuspicious of traps. And they much prefer to hunt their own food than to take meat or fish bait. Furthermore (*pace* the RSPCA), apart from the fact that cage traps can scarcely be described as 'humane', most people who set them are inclined to forget them, and mink have often been reported dead of stress and star-vation in such contraptions. Naturally a mink can be shot if you chance on one, but they are secretive creatures, rarely seen. Comparatively few suc-cumb to snare or trap, shotgun or rifle. No – the most effective means of control is the minkhound.

A minkhound may come of otterhound or foxhound stock or be a cross of the two. But any big strong hound of natural hunting tendency, and which is a bold swimmer, should enter well to mink. At the time of writing there are eighteen such packs in Britain, hunting under the auspices of the Masters of Minkhounds Association, which ordains that 'the quarry must be fairly hunted in its wild and natural state'. The season runs from April to the end of September, most hunts having their opening meet on the first Saturday in May. A mink hunt's chief source of information will be local farmers, gamekeepers or anglers, who have either seen mink or evidence of their activity. Hounds are taken to the river, stream or lake closest to the point at which the mink has been reported. They will then attempt to trace it, from its overnight drag, to where it is lying up. If it takes refuge in a tree it is shot.

The popularity of minkhunting has increased steadily ever since its beginnings and all those who observe the Countryside Code of responsible behaviour have been, and are, welcome at the meets. And, not unreasonably, the death of each and every mink is hailed as a minor triumph.

GAME SHOOTING

Colin Laurie McKelvie

Colin Laurie McKelvie is an independent publisher, specialising in wildlife and sporting books. He is also author of eight books on field sports and game conservation, and is a frequent contributor to sporting and wildlife magazines in Britain and Ireland. A Vice-Chancellor's Prizeman of Trinity College, Dublin and a chartered biologist, he was Britain's first Chief Wildlife Act Inspector and subsequently Director of Information and Publicity with The Game Conservancy Trust.

The term 'game' has a precise legal definition and also an accepted sporting meaning, and the two do not quite coincide. While the law defines game as those species of birds and mammals which are listed in the Game Act of 1831 and its subsequent amendments, sportsmen draw on a more widely and loosely assorted range of traditions and received ideas, many with remote historical origins. In the present consideration of the practice and influence of British game shooting, the term is taken to encompass not only those species legally designated game but also other legitimate quarry species of British farmland, uplands and inland marshes, such as woodpigeons, hares, rabbits, woodcock and snipe. (Deer are also game, and ducks and geese are important quarry species, but these are discussed elsewhere in this volume.)

Provided he has the necessary gun licence, a game licence and access to suitable land, any individual may go shooting game in season. But one of the distinctive characteristics of British game shooting is the essentially sociable and communal nature of the sport. The wildfowler, the rough shooter and the deer stalker may pursue their sport alone – and will often fare better by doing so – but a typical shooting day with pheasants or partridges on wooded farmland or with grouse on heather moorland involves the deployment of a team of guns and a supporting staff of beaters, gamekeepers, stops, flag-men, drivers and dog-handlers. Since the development of the breech-loading shotgun in the 1850s, most British game shooting has involved the driving of game birds over a line of standing guns, to provide them with testing shooting at fast, high quarry.

Individual sportsmen have personal preferences for certain sporting species and different styles of shooting, but there is general agreement that the touchstone of excellence lies in the presentation of mature, vigorous birds flying within humane killable range but at heights and speeds which constitute a stern test of the shooters' skills. In achieving this ideal much depends upon considerations such as the weather, the wind speed and direction, the lie of the land and the positioning of the guns; and the wise shoot organiser will be able to alter his procedures to accommodate changing conditions. This is especially applicable to driven pheasant shooting. One variable factor the host or shoot manager should bear in mind is the competence of the guns shooting on any particular day. A team of skilful and experienced guns may shoot accurately up to the limits of their shotguns' ballistic capabilities, and will also be able readily to identify birds which are too high or too far away to be shot cleanly, and which will therefore not be fired at. A weaker or less experienced team of guns should not be tested so severely, and their more modest skills may be pitted against birds presented at somewhat lower heights and in a way which a stronger team might find almost too easy. In this way responsible shoot organisation can minimise the risks of wounding birds while maintaining good sporting standards for the guns.

Certain areas of Britain, and certain game species in especially favourable habitats, can provide ample game shooting at purely wild birds. Red grouse, for example, are wholly wild and their presence and abundance is directly related to the availability of suitable heather moorland. Britain's highest grouse densities are found on the dry, well-keepered moors of northern England, with low numbers in much of north-west Scotland, Ireland and Wales, owing to poor habitat and insufficient keepering. Some parts of East Anglia, for example, are able to maintain high populations of wild pheasants and partridges, and there shoots are able to provide good sport without rearing and releasing any birds. In such well-favoured lowland areas the main thrust of game management is directed, as on the best grouse moors, towards the maintenance of good nesting and feeding habitat for the wild birds, and the minimising of predation, especially in spring when the birds are nesting.

Elsewhere, and more typically of most of the British Isles, local conditions make it essential for shoot managers to augment and support their populations of wild pheasants and partridges by annual release programmes. The unacceptable alternative would be a short-term period of excessive shooting pressure on the wild stock, followed by the almost total abandonment of game management on an area where shooting is no longer viable, in which case game species and wildlife in general would suffer from neglect. Properly done, releasing makes a major contribution, not only to sport but also to game management and wildlife conservation. A responsible rearing and releasing programme nurtures the pheasant's egg through the critically

vulnerable period from laying to the fledging of the young bird. Successively in the incubator, the brooder unit and the release pen, the developing embryo and the growing chick are secure from predation, starvation and the vagaries of the weather. The maturing poult is gradually habituated to life in the coverts on the shoot, and eventually adopts a wholly feral life in early autumn, by which time it should be a vigorous and elusive sporting bird, indistinguishable from its wild-bred cousins.

The supplementary feeding of reared game on a shoot, such as the provision of grain for pheasants to hold them in the coverts, also benefits wild game and various other species, especially in severe weather such as often occurs after the shooting season ends in February. Game strips, cover crops and berried shrubs planted for game also shelter and feed many other creatures, while carefully managed hedgerows and woodlands provide habitats for countless species of animals, birds, insects and plants. Environmentalists, whatever their personal reservations about the morality of field sports, are unanimous in agreeing that the planting of small woodlands primarily as game coverts has been hugely beneficial to the diversity of Britain's lowland landscape. Today, game shooting remains the single most important incentive for creating new mixed species plantations.

However, rearing and releasing, especially of pheasants, can lend itself to serious abuses, especially where shoots are run commercially. One reprehensible practice is to release excessive numbers of reared pheasants onto a limited acreage, perhaps augmenting them by periodic further releases after shooting has begun. This produces unnaturally high densities of pheasants, which then destroy whatever suitable habitat there may be, and the birds are given no time to develop the feral wiliness and strength of flight that makes them a sporting quarry. The misuse of releasing to generate the maximum commercial revenue from paying guns can thus lead to poor sport with inferior birds, insupportable shooting pressure on wild game stocks, and the general degradation of the land for all wildlife. The expansion of game shooting in the generally affluent years of the 1980s, especially in southern England, led to the development of many such shoots, often catering chiefly for business clients buying days' shooting as a form of corporate entertaining.

On commercial shoots with excessively large rearing programmes, and releasing throughout the season, there has been a tendency to shoot very large bags of pheasants. Most game shooters are familiar with persistent and repugnant reports of excessive bags of pheasants – perhaps 1,000 birds or more – being shot in one day under questionable conditions. These malpractices may even have been compounded by the wasteful destruction of the day's bag by burning or burying, owing to depressed game prices and the impossibility of selling large numbers of poorly conditioned birds. Such excesses were undoubtedly stimulated by a period of unusually high investment profits and a general stockmarket boom, and by 1988 it was evident that this form of commercially orientated shooting was already in decline, owing to a straitened financial climate and also in response to significant criticism from within game-shooting circles.

The various British shooting organisations, responding to and reflecting their members' disquiet, combined to produce *The Code of Good Shooting Practice*, in 1989. This enunciated the general principles of gun safety, sportsmanship, good shoot management and environmentally sound

sporting practices, and it constitutes the best public pronouncement on game shooting in modern times. The timing of its publication and the tenor of its advice for shoot management are both symptomatic of a significant groundswell of concern among game shooters that their sport should be seen to play a positive role in practical wildlife conservation.

Almost simultaneous with the promulgation of the *Code* was the publication of *Game 2000: a Manifesto for the Future of Game in Britain*, in the 1990s and beyond, issued by The Game Conservancy Trust. This expanded upon the *Code*'s necessarily brief recommendations about game conservation, and emphasised the benefits of enlightened game management for wildlife and the natural environment in general. It presented the case for encouraging intelligent game management and game shooting within the context of diversified land use, and for working towards a balanced conservation strategy which takes account of game species, their predators, and other forms of wildlife sharing the same environment. This important and well publicised voluntary initiative from within the game shooting community was widely applauded by conservationists, environmentalists and commentators in the press and broadcasting.

When game shooting is in progress, one of the principal tenets of good sportsmanship which should be conscientiously observed is that wounded game should be recovered and accounted for with minimum delay, and that strenuous efforts should be made to find and despatch any animal or bird known to have been hit. This should stem from three principal impulses – humanitarian concern; awareness of the public image of the sport; and the value, both symbolic and material, of the shot game. There is no reason to believe that contemporary game shooters are any less humane than were earlier generations, and there are very good grounds for crediting them with a share in the heightened awareness of animal welfare which prevails among western cultures today. Game shooting must be humane and be seen to be so, and modern field sportsmen are conscious as never before of the need to maintain and improve an acceptable public profile.

Although the serious slump in game prices since the mid-1980s has diminished the financial incentive to recover every bird shot, there remains an important tradition of respect for dead quarry, which has its roots in very ancient hunting practices. Although British sportsmen do not practice the elaborate and stylised rituals of their counterparts in Continental Europe, most game shoots implement important, but simple, practical measures to ensure that shot game, having been quickly retrieved and promptly despatched, is methodically hung up or laid out so as to keep it cool, dry, attractive to see and hygienic to eat. These principles of prompt gathering and humane dispatch apply equally to the solitary pigeon shooter flighting birds in a wood or shooting over decoys on a field of rape, who should send his dog to retrieve all birds without delay.

Traditionally, picking up dead and wounded game birds was a task assigned to estate or shoot staff, perhaps assisted by one or two gundog trainers and handlers preparing dogs to compete in field trials. However, since the 1970s picking up has developed into something of a minor field sport in its own right, regularly practised by a growing number of enthusiasts who are neither professional gundog trainers nor field trial competitors, but who find picking up a satisfying and testing way of handling a working gundog. This is a welcome trend, and the availability of a sufficient number of good retrieving dogs, worked by capable handlers, minimises the chances of wounded game being left to suffer, or dead game not being recovered. Few British shoots will find much difficulty in securing the help of a number of such locally resident volunteer pickers-up, who should be encouraged to attend shoots regularly, thereby acquiring a useful familiarity with the lie of the land and the quirks of individual drives and beats.

Accurate shooting, achieved and maintained by regular practice, minimises the incidence of wounding, and every shooter of live quarry should strive to attain a high standard of accuracy and to recognise his personal limitations if he is to derive full satisfaction from his sport and shoot humanely as good sportsmanship requires. Since the late 1960s numerous new cartridge manufacturers have entered the British market, offering wide choice in a market previously dominated by one or two suppliers. Consequently, the price of shotgun cartridges has remained relatively static, and has fallen in real terms. At the same time scores of clay-pigeon shooting layouts and commercially run shooting schools have opened in many parts of the United Kingdom. Easy access to shooting grounds and expert professional coaching, together with the ready availability of modestly priced cartridges, has made it possible for the modern game shooter to practice regularly by shooting clay pigeons. A considerable number of guns now do this as a prelude to the opening of a new shooting season, and to help improve their general standard of shooting. This trend is to be applauded, as are any measures which make the shooter of live quarry more alert, discriminating and accurate – and therefore more humane.

Despite the sociable nature of organised game shooting, most British shooters have been curiously reluctant to join their representative organisations or to play a part in their activities. There may be something in our national character which makes us generally disinclined to allow our personal pleasures in sport and recreation to become regimented or centrally co-ordinated. However, since the 1950s, and increasingly rapidly since the 1970s, there has been a steady trend towards support of the voluntary organisations representing game shooting and game shooters. The membership of the two principal voluntary organisations catering for the game shooter has greatly increased since the early 1980s. That of The Game Conservancy Trust doubled from 10,000 to 20,000 in the five years from 1984 to 1989, while that of the British Association for Shooting and Conservation increased by over thirty per cent to almost 100,000 during the same period. This does not reflect a proportionate increase in the numbers of active shooters of game and live quarry, although that plays a small part in the equation. It does reveal, however, that shooters have become increasingly willing to support these organisations. It is significant that their names and charters indicate that both are concerned with the conservation of shooters' quarry, its habitat, and thus the wider natural environment. Indeed, The Game Conservancy Trust is Britain's only organisation devoted primarily to scientific research into game species and the development of practical game management techniques, for which it receives no government funding. Britain is unique among the world's developed countries in having no state-funded organisation charged with overseeing the management of game species, and it is a significant and welcome development that British sportsmen should themselves have created and financed such an organisation.

Education – of the shooter, the shoot manager and the general public – is a high priority of the representative shooting organisations in Britain and Ireland. They recognise that the traditional sport of game shooting is highly susceptible to misunderstanding and vulnerable to attack in a society whose opinion-makers and mass media of information, although increasingly out of touch with the quotidien realities of rural life and recreation, are neverthe-less eager to have an influential voice in countryside, wildlife, and environ-mental affairs. They also feel that game shooting and game management

have an important record of practical achievements in wildlife conservation, in which the husbandry of game for sport has involved sportsmen and landowners in a concomitant and inseparable stewardship of British wildlife in general. The traditional and continuing solicitude of the sportsman for the future wellbeing of his quarry, for its habitat and, by extension, for the countless species which share it, is perceived by the shooting community as a role for which it has in the past received little credit from environmentalists. Since the 1970s this situation has changed; game managers have been ready to proclaim and demonstrate their conservation role with growing energy and effectiveness, and there has emerged a new breed of pragmatic ecologists who are increasingly ready to acknowledge the environmental importance of land-management strategies in which game shooting plays a part.

Among environmentalists game shooting is increasingly acknowledged to exert a generally beneficial influence upon the management of farmland. Hedgerows, which might otherwise be removed, are retained and managed to provide gamebirds with nesting habitat and cover; and small woodlands have been created and maintained principally for their game potential, and with great collateral benefits to many other species of birds, mammals, insects and plants. On open farmland in Britain the indigenous and formerly abundant grey partridge has declined catastrophically since the 1950s, and research has proved this to be directly caused by degradation or total loss of the habitat of fields and hedgerows, the profligate use of chemical sprays and the widespread cessation of traditional predation control, especially at the spring nesting season. Where these three cardinal changes have been avoided, partridge populations generally remain buoyant, and many species of wild flowers, insects, butterflies and small birds also abound. It is now recognised that landscapes which sustain large numbers of wild game birds are also rich in countless other forms of wildlife.

Especially prominent in the public discussion of the British countryside and its wildlife has been the general recognition that the management of heather moorland for grouse shooting is the chief bastion which maintains Britain's unique upland ecosystem against degradation and destruction caused by livestock, overgrazing and commercial afforestation. The press and broadcasting media, formerly notorious for their flippantly dismissive coverage of the opening of the grouse shooting season on 12th August, now increasingly use this annual event as an occasion for serious and well-informed discussion of the ecological plight of ill-managed moorland, and much of the credit for this trend goes to the energetic campaigns of public information and education promoted by the shooting organisations. Their public information role has stressed the value of careful land management, the continuity of private ownership and the careful regulation of shooting, and has made an especially valuable contribution to the

continuing environmental and land-use debate at a time when private landowners, the National Trust and central government are all under growing pressure to facilitate unlimited public recreational access to the countryside in general and the uplands in particular, with all the pressures of disturbance, erosion and pollution which that would bring to bear upon wildlife and the landscape.

In Britain the formal education of game-shooters, especially newcomers to the sport, and also of gamekeepers and shoot managers, was unknown until very recently, for the traditions and skills of sportsmanship and the arts and crafts of the gamekeeper were handed on informally from one generation to another. Today, expert and regular regional tuition, within structured meetings and residential courses, is widely available through the advisory service of The Game Conservancy and the BASC, and these are growing in popularity. Such courses and tutorials are both intensive and extensive in scope, encompassing topics as diverse as gun safety, shooting etiquette, sporting law, practical game biology, habitat management and humane shoot organisation. Guest lecturers include ecologists, the police and animal welfare experts. Those involved in modern game shooting therefore have ready access to sound education and expert, broadly based guidance, unknown to their predecessors. Following this valuable lead given by the voluntary organisations, several British agricultural colleges now offer full-time game management training courses.

It is understandable that game species, and especially the principal game birds such as pheasants, grouse and partridges, excite powerful loyalties

and enthusiasms among game shooters, but this is not mirrored by any comparable interest on the part of the general public. Indeed, in the 1970s a poll of members of the Royal Society for the Protection of Birds actually indicated that the pheasant was the British bird they liked least of all! But aesthetic considerations apart, game like pheasants are also a potentially important source of excellent meat, and yet there is pitifully little general public interest in game as food. Housewives and others shopping for meat and poultry in the principal retail outlets such as supermarkets tend not to buy game for the table, despite strenuous efforts by game dealers and others to promote it. In Britain consumer resistance to game remains high, fuelled by a general unfamiliarity with wild foods of every kind in an increasingly urbanised society; by the absence of any significant British tradition of game cuisine; and by potential buyers' wariness of a seemingly exotic form of food. The bulk of game shot in Britain is therefore exported to foreign markets such as the countries of northern Europe, and what little is retained is largely consumed either by those associated with game shooting or by the patrons of expensive restaurants.

The present low status of shot game, and therefore its low market value, could be greatly enhanced if the consumption of game and game products were promoted more effectively, and much of the responsibility for doing this falls upon sportsmen, shoot managers and game dealers. Today, an increasingly fruitful line of persuasion is the promotion of game as a healthy, natural, and 'organic' form of protein, low in saturated fats, virtually devoid of additives and agrochemicals, and rich in flavour. Success in promoting game in the national diet would enhance not only the value of shot game but also the esteem in which game creatures, game habitats and game management are held, to the eventual benefit of wildlife conservation in general.

Finally, it is important to remember that, to shoot game, or to 'kill or take game' by any means, the law requires that the individual shall have an appropriate game licence, costing £12 for one year. Unlike the licensing arrangements in most of Europe, North America and Africa, this levy is not used to finance any form of game or wildlife conservation but merely goes into the Treasury's consolidated fund. Despite the solitary but significant precedent established by the levy on horserace betting, in which money is ploughed back into the sport, the British Treasury is opposed in principle to the hypothecation of any tax for a specific purpose. Game conservation in the United Kingdom therefore receives no state funding, and the legal requirement to hold a game licence is widely disregarded among game shooters and rarely enforced by the police, being generally viewed as a rather risible anachronism, almost on a par with the old and discredited system of dog licensing. There is no doubt that many more game shooters would be prepared to buy licences if the funds thus generated were seen directly to benefit game and wildlife. The experience of other countries indicates that the greatest single contribution the British government could make to game conservation would be to plough game licence revenues back into research and practical management, preferably under the aegis of an expert independent agency such as The Game Conservancy Trust. Such a logical yet imaginative move would be welcomed by sportsmen and informed conservationists alike.

WILDFOWLING

Arthur Cadman

The son of a celebrated landowning breeder of Dexter cattle, Arthur Cadman was educated at Malvern and at Oxford, where he took his degree in forestry, and from which he went on to serve for thirty-four years with the Forestry Commission, a period that included the post of Deputy Surveyor of the New Forest. On retirement he started a shrub and heather nursery and a game advisory service. An acknowledged expert on the conservation of both waterfowl and deer and, for eleven years, manager of the goose shooting on the Loch of Strathbeg, Arthur Cadman was awarded the OBE for 'voluntary work for the conservation of wildlife'.

Man has always been a hunter. He had to be to live and in the beginning the main quarry species were the larger animals, bear, boar, deer and other animals of the area where he lived. Wildfowling too was an early need. But, gradually, there became a division amongst those who pursued ducks, geese and waders. First, there were the professionals, who made their living from the fowl they netted, trapped or shot. They lived a hard life, exposed to all weathers, and they had to be out and about by day and by night. Often, despite great skill and knowledge of the fowl they hunted, their bag would be empty. They did their wildfowling between high and low water on British shores, among the samphire and sea lavender of the saltmarshes, or out on the mud of the estuaries. In those early days, apart from close seasons, the protection for rare birds was minimal. There was a keen market for taxidermy, and the motto of the longshoreman was: 'What's hit is history: What's missed is mystery!' They contributed much to the knowledge, incidence and distribution of very many species, from bluethroats to spoonbills.

The other wildfowler was the gentleman amateur, who shot geese and ducks for sport. This, too, was a hard sport, often with little reward other than the magic of wild places and the call of the birds that lived there. Very great names come to mind: Colonel Peter Hawker, Charles St John, Sir Ralph Payne Gallwey, Abel Chapman, J. G. Millais, Stanley Duncan, Jeffrey Harrison, Christopher Dalgety, Sir Peter Scott and many others. All these great naturalist-wildfowlers were writers on the subject and much accurate information became available from their careful observations, for shooting and ornithology went hand-in-hand.

Peter Hawker left us *Instructions To Young Sportsmen*; Charles St John wrote a wealth of fine observations. His illustration (1852) depicts the first accurate record of a Greenland whitefront goose (the whitefront of Scotland) which was not formally recorded until 1947, nearly a hundred years later, when Peter Scott and Christopher Dalgety identified this race. (Charles St John unwittingly explains a common error of those early days, when pink-feet were recorded as bean geese. His illustration of a pink, recorded as a bean, is on the same page as the Greenland whitefront.) Sir Ralph Payne-Gallwey's *The Fowler in Ireland* (1882) is another great work. Abel Chapman wrote *Wild Spain* and it was he who recorded the first lesser whitefront in Britain. J. G. Millais wrote *The Wildfowler in Scotland*, and his other writings and collections of birds are famous. Stanley Duncan wrote many articles. It was through his foresight that WAGBI was formed in 1908 (the Wildfowl Association of Great Britain and Ireland). In 1981 the name was changed to the BASC (British Association for Shooting and Conservation), a fine organisation which every shooting man should support.

Dr Jeffrey Harrison, of International repute, represented the British government on the Ramsar Convention of Wetlands and Waterfowl. He wrote a number of books and was responsible for much scientific research. Christopher Dalgety wrote *Wildfowling* and many articles and Sir Peter Scott, whose superb paintings and enormous work for conservation, are known world-wide, founded the Wildfowl Trust. I have mentioned these great names because nothing illustrates better the affinity between the great sport of wildfowling and scientific knowledge.

Those mentioned were all puntgunners. This is, in my opinion, the greatest sport in Britain and unfortunately it is much maligned, but little understood. Briefly, a punt gunner in a single-handed punt, or two in a double punt, set forth to stalk wildfowl in a very shallow craft (which is not well-designed for rough water). The sport should be practiced under relatively calm conditions. There have been serious accidents when bad storms occur. The punt is armed with a heavy gun of $1^3/_4''$ bore. The successful shot is taken at a bunch of wildfowl at sixty yards. On average a shot is obtained once in three outings, which may last twelve hours, as one goes out on the ebb tide and comes back on the flood tide. The average kill is ten ducks and it is rare for even one to escape, because the shallow punt can follow over water and the puntsman can pursue a wounded duck with a cripple stopper across mud or sand. There is nowhere on such a place for a duck to hide and a dog is not required.

Compare a big punt shot of, say, twenty ducks with a similar bag made by two or three shore shooters. On average they will use some sixty cartridges to bag twenty ducks. Of the forty ineffective shots nearly half may have touched the target, leaving, say, fifteen ducks with an odd pellet in them. Which sport is the most efficient? Punt gunning is too often condemned through sheer ignorance. It is the most difficult stalking sport in Britain, requiring a very high degree of skill and physical fitness.

The formation of WAGBI by Stanley Duncan was a great step forward in the attitude to wildfowl and conservation. Although conservation was not included in the title until it was changed to BASC, it became a major influence in the outlook of wildfowlers.

One of the greatest needs for the conservation of all species of geese is peace and quiet on the roosts. If geese are shot on the roost, then they have to move elsewhere, and the goose population of a whole estuary may disappear. WAGBI, through the knowledge of their members, knew where the major roosts were. The association co-operated with the NCC (Nature Conservancy Council) in the establishment of Reserves where they were needed. These were developed over the years, so the standard of behaviour on the shore improved, and clubs did much local conservation work.

It is a sad fact that, because a wild goose is regarded as the elite quarry of all wildfowl species, selfish greed and bad behaviour began to be experienced on the shore. The culprits (a small minority but of ever-increasing numbers) who enjoy the sport of wildfowling, are despised by all true wildfowlers, and soon earned the name of 'marsh cowboys'. The wildfowl clubs developed their own rules for sporting behaviour. Young members were trained in the tradition of sportsmanship and they were taught to identify their quarry, to learn the effective killing range of their weapon, and, in short, to respect the fowl they shot, as well as the other users of the shore. Today members of the BASC are in the forefront of upholding the etiquette and the traditions of wildfowling.

However, there are still some 'marsh cowboys'. These individuals, including some foreigners from countries where even small songbirds are the normal quarry, continue to bring the good name of wildfowlers into

disrepute. It is the case that a man who would behave perfectly well on his home beat often behaves badly elsewhere. He may be carried away by the excitement of the chase when shooting geese. Geese are big birds. They look to be nearer than they are, and the most common fault is to shoot at them at excessive range, partly through ignorance, partly in the hope that a fluke shot may bring down a goose.

Greed, in the form of trying to use the best place, ignoring the interests of local people and, sometimes, poaching geese on private land, is another form of unacceptable behaviour. Sometimes visitors from away have no idea how to conceal themselves and by standing upright, or walking about during a flight, they cause untold disturbance. That may save the lives of geese, but it does nothing for the peace of mind of the local club members who behave properly. Sometimes excessive bags are shot, something of which a local fowler would not be guilty.

It is necessary to highlight this bad behaviour. It is up to everyone to do his best to put an end to it. Luckily, as already said, it is a small minority who behave thus, and they are rightly despised, and condemned. Too much must not be made of this. There are 'bad hats' in every community. That the sporting behaviour of shooting people is far more responsible than is that of many other people who indulge in sports, where no lethal weapons are available, may be seen at any Game Fair – the greatest annual event for all shooting people.

At Game Fairs the major banks are represented by temporary mobile banks. One major event is the clay-pigeon shooting, where thousands of rounds are fired. Young men, carrying their guns in sleeves, may be seen passing to and fro into the banks. Yet, apart from traffic police, it is unusual to see more than half-a-dozen policemen on the whole site. Compare this with any major football match where there are no banks and no (legal) weapons, but where supervision by police costs thousands of pounds and arrests of hooligans are frequent. Most shooting people are responsible, and the difficulties imposed by recent legislation, making it more difficult to own a rifle or a shot gun, are considered by many shooting people to have been heavyhanded.

Let us now consider some of the benefits that have been gained from the sport of wildfowling and duck shooting. A wildfowler harvests a valuable natural resource. Almost any creature, if allowed to increase uncontrolled, will eventually become too numerous to exist on the food of its natural habitat. Then nature steps in with starvation and disease. There is a crash in numbers, and it may take many years for healthy levels to creep back. Ducks and geese have few predators in their winter habitats and by taking much of the annual increase, a healthy breeding stock remains.

It is a fact that, despite a curtailment of wetlands through reclamation for agriculture, despite more wildfowlers, and a great increase in non-shooting

human pressures, the numbers of all the major quarry species of ducks and geese, which winter on these shores, have either increased, or been maintained. Where some of the more rare species become at risk, the wildfowler is the first to co-operate in having the species put on the protected list. Unfortunately the same co-operation is notable by its absence, when a quarry species is given protection and increases to a point where it is no longer in need of protection, the dark-bellied brent goose for example.

The dark-bellied brent is a bird of the shore, feeding mainly on a marine grass (three species of zostera). The zostera went into a decline probably due to a bacterial disease, influenced by oil spills and the brent goose numbers fell drastically. It was given full protection in 1954. It was not until (many years later) this goose began to feed, like grey geese, inside the sea wall, that their numbers began to increase. The good food of grass and wheat meant that breeding geese returned to their breeding-grounds in good condition. Numbers began to recover. Now, despite occasional climatic disasters on the summer haunts, this goose is as numerous as the greylag and the pinkfoot. Yet the brent is still protected, despite considerable damage done to farmers. That is a bone of contention with wildfowlers and a loss of a good food resource, for brent which have been feeding on grass or cereal shoots are very good to eat.

Another important development is the Hard Weather Ban. Hard weather brings many inland ducks to the shore and it has always been regarded as the prime wildfowling time. But prolonged hard weather imposes a heavy strain on wildfowl and may cause loss of weight and, ultimately, death. All parties agree that, at such times, a ban on shooting is necessary. Wildfowlers have played a leading role in producing a formula which the Home Secretary and Secretary of State for Scotland use as a basis to bring in a legal ban. It is the case that the imposition of this ban may impose some apparently unfair discrimination against wildfowlers who live near an estuary which has escaped the hard weather. They should accept this in the interests of all. The hard weather stress on wildfowl may be serious due to shortage of food because of ice or snow. Here again those surplus numbers, already shot, will benefit those that remain, when food is in very short supply.

Wildfowling clubs often offer a service to adjoining estates whereby they control crows, magpies and foxes. Some have their own reserves as breeding ponds. Geese do damage to farmland. Sometimes the damage is serious. To some extent scaring is effective, but shooting is more so. Despite increased shooting, goose numbers are still increasing. With no shooting there would be a goose population explosion with serious consequences.

Of course inland wildfowlers and duck shooters do a great deal for conservation. A good duck shoot is only shot at infrequent periods – say once a month. In between it is kept free from any disturbance and when it freezes the ice is broken. A great deal of food is supplied and, on average, not more than ten per cent of the ducks using the area are shot. So ninety per cent benefit from the food and freedom from disturbance. The greatest benefit of all comes after the season ends. Feeding is continued and the very important reason for this is to help breeding ducks to reach the breeding season in good condition. Those that are about to face the heavy strain of migration are in tip-top condition, too. The females that have benefited in this way tend to bring their offspring back to the water which they left in the spring.

Small flight ponds, heavily fed, take a much heavier toll than that ten per cent, but most of the duck shot on these ponds are mallard, which are not in short supply. Indeed large numbers are reared. These small flight ponds are invaluable in another way. They provide a habitat for vast numbers of

creatures – frogs, toads, newts, crustacea and water insect and plant life. Dragonflies benefit especially. So much of Britain's marshes and wetlands have been drained, often uneconomically, that any ponds or marshes which are maintained as such have a special part to play in the survival of much pond life.

Another great advantage to wildlife on and around big estates, comes from the gamekeeping which takes place there. Foxes, rats, crows and magpies do serious damage to ducks and ducklings. But they also do much damage to many other species, not connected with shooting at all. Magpies and jays are particularly harmful to small birds' eggs and young. Indeed the recent increase of magpie numbers is one of the reasons for the decline of so many passerine species. Crows devastate many ground-nesting birds, especially waders. One of the main reasons why the Cley Marshes Reserve, managed so well by the Norfolk Naturalists' Trust, is so successful is that crows, foxes and rats are continually controlled. Some of the Reserves run by other organisations suffer severe losses. In 1990 it was reported that 300 Little tern nests were destroyed by predators on one RSPB Reserve. If that is so, it is an unacceptable loss. One man, taking one egg, would be prosecuted (rightly so), but what about the person who let 300 nests be destroyed? A wildfowl club would never allow such a terrible loss!

The new EEC proposed legislation to give protection to crows and magpies during their breeding season is an astonishing piece of nonsense. It may be possible to get over this by the issue of licences for their control, but that only leads to bureaucratic muddle. It will be amazing if such legislation is allowed to come about. Britain has an Oceanic climate totally different from that of the Continent. Here much of the land over 1,500 feet above sea level is moorland, where thousands of waders, and other birds, including ducks and grouse, breed. Land of the same elevation in Germany, for instance, is mainly forest. Very few ground-nesting birds occur there. The most valued species to occupy this land are deer and boar and therefore there is no incentive to control crows and magpies. Our own Countryside and Wildlife Act of 1981 is a fine example of the sort of legislation that is required. Indeed, on the matter of game laws and wildlife protection, Britain has been to the forefront since legislation was first undertaken.

I must refer to one other very important matter in relation to wildfowl. Although knowledge of ducks and geese, their habitat requirements, their migration routes, and breeding habits, and much else, has advanced greatly in the last twenty years, there is still an enormous amount to be learnt. Scientific research and practical wildfowling must go hand in hand. One important line of research was investigated by Jeffrey Harrison, before his sad death. That concerned the information which a study of duck wings can provide. Wildfowlers have sent in thousands of wings from duck which they have shot. From this study, breeding success each year, the proportion of the sexes, even different movements of young and old, male and female, and much else have been discovered. It is the practical wildfowler on the shore, who can best provide the scientist with many of the facts he needs.

Finally I would make a plea for better co-operation between the conservationist, who does not shoot, and the wildfowler, who is normally just as keen a conservationist. If he was not so his shooting might suffer – but that is not the main reason for his interest. His motive is a love of the shore birds and the quarry species and a love, too, of the wild places they inhabit.

What would be the result for the countryside if wildfowling were to be banned? The most serious effect would be the loss of much wetland habitat. Salt marshes, fresh water marshes and ponds would be drained. Wildfowlers form a very powerful body. Without their opposition to development and reclamation many wetland areas, and the enormous amount of wildlife which they support, would be lost. Already the decline of such areas has had a devastating effect on wildlife. Our wetlands cannot stand many more major losses, such for example, as barrages to harness some of our most important estuaries. Further losses would have a very serious effect upon the thousands of waders which winter on our shores. The politicians' farcical answer: 'Oh they'll go elsewhere' shows a crass ignorance. If there was an 'elsewhere' it would be fully occupied already. Nature does not tolerate empty areas. Some species of duck would experience a large population increase. Without the partial control of numbers, a hard winter would see huge losses through starvation. In some areas, like the Cambridge Washes, disease through overcrowding would occur. In warm weather botulism would be likely.

The effect upon goose numbers would be the most devastating. The grey geese (greylag and pinkfoot) and Canada geese are already considered to be too numerous in many areas. A population explosion would cause very serious winter and spring damage to agriculture and there would be no means to alleviate this – other than shooting under licence, a very unsatisfactory and ineffective solution. In some areas on the shore, brent geese and wigeon would eat out much of the zostera beds, and damage by brent geese, along with the grey geese, would continue to increase. The incentive to control crows and magpies on vast areas of marshland would no longer exist. The increase in corvids would have a serious effect upon waders and many other species. Commercially there would be a serious effect upon the gun trade and on those who supply specialised shooting equipment. Some of the rural economy would be affected, because there would be no winter visitors to fill hotels and lodgings (at a time when such trade is extra important).

There is another not so obvious point. Wildfowling is a healthy sport. It provides a useful spare-time occupation for many people and there is a strong school of thought that the more young people are involved in healthy outdoor sport, the less vandalism and hooliganism there will be. In short it is a healthy outlet for the 'hunting instinct' referred to at the start of this chapter.

STALKING

Richard Prior

Richard Prior was educated at Bryanston School and subsequently trained in farming and agricultural engineering. He joined the Forestry Commission in 1962, specialising in forest damage, deer control methods and stalker training. In 1977 he was appointed information director and deer consultant to The Game Conservancy, six years later becoming an independent deer consultant with close affiliations with both the British Deer Society and The Game Conservancy. In 1976 he was awarded the Balfour Browne award for deer conservation; and, in 1989, won a Churchill Travelling Fellowship, in the same context, to Poland and Siberia. He is the author of eleven books on deer and stalking.

A UNIQUE WILDLIFE RESOURCE

Deer of six different species are very widely distributed over most of the United Kingdom. The population is impossible to assess but probably exceeds one million. In this respect Britain has a wildlife resource unique in Europe, both in density and diversity. We are often confronted by alarming accounts of 'disappearing wildlife'. The *Red Book* gives details of endangered species. Pollution, urbanisation and all the other threats to the countryside are so graphically displayed that the ability of such large animals as deer to live successfully in close proximity to man is difficult to accept. Yet while most species of birds are in decline throughout Europe, deer have increased to a point where they have probably never been so numerous.

Deer are, it must be realized, typical prey species. They are designed to be eaten and have in consequence a comparatively high reproductive rate. Over the centuries, we have eliminated all large predators, such as the wolf, the bear and the lynx. Nothing remains to control deer numbers but starvation and disease, or the actions of man. The deerstalker's argument is that he acts as a substitute for the wolf. If he does his job well, he keeps the deer population as healthy as it would have been when regularly preyed upon. In addition, a rifle bullet well directed is more humane than being hamstrung and pulled down by wolves, or dying slowly by starvation as a natural control of over-population.

Being tender-hearted on this issue would be the cruellest solution of all. As it is, a significant number of deer perish each year because we are not yet controlling the herds sufficiently to limit their increase to within the carrying capacity of their range.

As well as considering their own welfare, one has to admit that large numbers of deer create serious problems to farmers and foresters (not to mention gardeners) because of the damage they do. Allowing Nature to control numbers by starvation would quickly result in quite intolerable damage in our intensively-cultivated and densely-populated island. Within the needs of balancing the presence of deer with other priorities of land use, the modern deerstalker summarises his aims of management in this way: to keep damage to an acceptable level; to keep the deer population healthy and in balance with food and cover available; to balance expenditure by harvesting a crop, in terms of venison, sport and recreation (deer watching, photography etc.). Deerstalking is thus the active tool of management. Most British stalkers, while enjoying their sport, make an honest attempt at deer conservation in these terms – a harvest of nutritious low-fat meat, organically grown, is a valuable by-product. The way deer are outwitted by the stalker depends on the species involved, the environment in which they live and a thorough understanding of their habits.

A HISTORY

Since Medieval times red and fallow deer were preserved for hunting, which ensured their survival in parts of the populous south. The New Forest and Exmoor, both Medieval Royal hunting reserves, are notable examples. In Scotland red deer have been highly regarded and managed as a sporting asset for nearly 200 years. The population there is now more than 300,000. Woodland-loving roe deer, like red deer, are native to this country. During the Middle Ages they became very scarce, but have increased enormously over the last 100 years. Wherever suitable habitat exists, it is likely that the whole of England, Wales and Scotland will be colonised by the year 2000. This success is due in part to reintroductions during the nineteenth century, but also to changes in the countryside, principally increased afforestation, which has been advantageous to them.

From the time of Domesday Book and before, wild deer were captured to be kept and bred in parks, either as a convenient food resource, for ornament, or, again, for sport. The old 'park pales' or cleft oak fences were always a nightmare to maintain, and escapes were commonplace. Added to this, in times of national commotion, deer parks were either pillaged or allowed to decay, from Cromwell's time to the two World Wars of our own century. The result is a healthy feral deer population. Fallow and red deer were the principal escapees, but they have been joined in this century by sika, muntjac and the antler-less Chinese water deer.

TRADITIONAL DEERSTALKING

To an earlier generation, deerstalking meant the pursuit of wild red deer in the Scottish Highlands. From the second quarter of the nineteenth century a vogue for this sport led to the preservation on behalf of the deer of a large part of the high moorland and mountain areas of the north, either exclusively, or in conjunction with grouse shooting and salmon fishing where the terrain and climate allowed. Crofting and larger-scale farming continued on the marginal land, while varying numbers of sheep and cattle continued to share what grazing was available on the open hill during the summer.

Following the lead of Queen Victoria, whose love of Scotland's wild places led to the acquisition of Balmoral, large tracts of hill land were purchased with the proceeds of nineteenth century industrial prosperity. They are known as deer forests, though much of the land is likely to be treeless. Large and comfortable lodges, some of them virtual mansions, were built in the wilds and liberally staffed, creating a vital new source of employment at a time when the Highlands had suffered a long period of social disruption and deprivation. Money was poured, and continues to be poured, into these remote areas because of the popularity of deerstalking, though the luxurious living of Edwardian houseparties has largely disappeared.

Roughly three million acres are designated as deer forest, though many other activities are either encouraged or tolerated by the forest owners, from rock climbing and mountain walking to skiing. Farming and crofting continue, supported by subsidies. On the lower slopes much land, previously open hill and used by the deer for wintering ground, has been fenced away for forestry. It is not difficult to suppose in these days of agricultural decline that even more of this hill land, the last great natural wilderness in Europe, would have been planted up if it were not for deerstalking.

Highland red deer live in a savage environment; poor impoverished soil, high rainfall, snow and frost in winter, tormenting insects in summer. They have developed an astonishing capacity to survive and to utilise low-quality forage with an efficiency unrivalled in any domestic animal. Stalking is sharply divided between stags and hinds. Stag stalking takes place in the autumn and attracts many sportsmen from overseas. Usually they are guided by a professional stalker. No matter how experienced the visitor may be, he needs the stalker's intimate knowledge of the ground. Alone, he may see deer, but he is all too likely to alarm them and even drive them temporarily off the forest altogether.

Hind stalking involves hard work, often under the worst weather conditions between mid-October and mid-February. Some redoubtable owners, tenants and paying guests brave the elements to take their part in this essential harvest. Otherwise the professional stalkers are left to get as many as they can, up to an agreed figure. The total population can only be controlled by reducing the number of breeding females. If too few are shot, the food supply will be insufficient for survival, and deer will die, sometimes in considerable numbers in the cold, comfortless days of early spring. There is also a vicious circle, for poorly-conditioned hinds will not breed until their fourth year, so a large proportion of non-breeders have to be carried for a breeding success which may be as low as sixteen per cent. The same deer in the relative abundance and warmth of forest conditions will start to breed at two years, and nearly every hind will have a calf annually.

In 1990, the population of red deer in Scotland was estimated to consist of more than 200,000 hinds and calves, but only 86,000 stags. This indicates the relative popularity and value of stag stalking which has led to over-exploitation of mature males, but also the regrettable tendency of the stags to roam. When they maraud on to farm or forestry land they are deprived of the protection which the deer forests offer, and many are shot out of season. The more the sex ratio is biased towards hinds, the more the stags roam. Hind stalking is a true wild sport, with every chance loaded against the stalker and is vitally necessary for the wellbeing of the deer herds. It is, however, neglected and under-exploited.

Scottish deerstalking has few parallels. In most parts of the world deer are active only at dawn and dusk. In the Highlands they can be seen, studied and stalked throughout the day. During the rut, in September and October, the stags' roaring echoes round the wild, rocky fastnesses of their home. Unless he has a distance to drive, the visitor to the hill (known as 'the Rifle') sets out with his professional guide (the Stalker) after a leisurely breakfast. A start may be made up the hill in a battered Land Rover, but sooner or later the party has to rely on legwork to gain height. It is rough walking, and anyone who has neglected his training soon starts to suffer. A considerate Stalker, seeing his guest's state, will soon settle down to spy the hill above for deer. A series of further climbs and spying sessions inevitably follows.

An experienced but urban-based Rifle knows that the first three days are the worst. After this his muscles gain strength, and he starts to appreciate the silence, the pure mountain air and the exhilarating feeling of being on the high tops. Equally, there is little to rival the utter luxury of a steaming, peaty bath, and maybe some of the wine of the country, at the end of a day which has tested the limits of his endurance. While part of the Stalker's task is to pinpoint deer and, by devious means, get his Rifle within range of a stag, he has the responsibility of selecting an animal for culling, which is either in poor condition, shows signs of being bad breeding stock, or has reached an age when his value to the herd is over.

In complete contrast to the trophy-hunter, who values his sport by the size of the stag's antlers which he has shot, Highland deerstalking measures success in memories. A difficult crawl; a group of suspicious hinds circumvented; a distant gleam of sunshine bringing vivid colour to an autumn-tinted rowan or patch of lichen; the company of a Stalker who is willing to talk about the mysteries and trials of his lonely life; and, above all, the final satisfaction of producing a beast for the larder which has been well-chosen for the good of the herd, and with a bullet in the right place for an instant and humane kill. If he is lucky, his stag may still be carried home on the back of a sturdy pony, or Garron. There are few more picturesque or satisfying sights than the jolting silhouette of a stag perched on the deer saddle, homeward bound after a good stalk.

Little is wasted of this harvest of the hills. The stag is paunched or gralloched where he falls, to the benefit of the ravens and other scavengers. The carcase is collected by the venison dealer, and the proceeds go some way towards defraying the heavy costs of running the forest. Most is exported, though people in Britain are starting to appreciate the qualities of wild-deer venison, free as it is of all artificial taints or drugs. As marketing and presentation improves, the home market is overcoming a resistance which dates back to the days of slow rail transport and meat which arrived in the south little better than carrion.

The sport of Highland deerstalking is a vital industry in itself. In addition to the stalker, ponyman or ghillie, who accompany the Rifle on the hill, each stag represents a value of approximately £40 to the local rates. Hotels, souvenir and clothes shops enjoy a longer season. There will be a gunmaker in the local town; a venison dealer, a saddler, a blacksmith and a garage – all this in areas with a short summer, poor communications and little other work.

WOODLAND STALKING

Although it is said that William the Conqueror 'loved the tall (red) deer as if he had been their father', wild deer of other species had few friends until recently. Roe and fallow, muntjac and sika were already present in pest proportions before we had any established tradition of management, or indeed the will to treat them with much respect. In the last century, deer in the lowlands were few. The enormous increase which has been a phenomenon of the last eighty years can probably be put down to the depopulation of the countryside and heavy woodland felling in both World Wars, followed by forestry programmes which commenced in 1919 and still continue.

Deer were legally snared until 1963, and large-scale drives to shotguns the normal response to over-population and damage. Except in very skilled hands and special situations, the shotgun is more likely to wound than kill. While a few enthusiasts stalked roe with the rifle between the wars, enthusiasm for woodland stalking as a sport in its own right only became generally accepted after 1945, mostly among servicemen who had had a taste of it in

Germany or Austria during the years immediately following the Second World War. They set out to prove that these pests had a right to better treatment than the indiscriminate snare or wounding shot pellet, and that control could be achieved effectively and humanely with the rifle. From the outset their approach was one of biological management, without any question of either maintaining an artificially high population, or of favouring the Continental tradition of trophy production.

The first aim had to be to change the status of deer from pests to animals which would be appreciated for their beauty and managed rather than persecuted. Fundamentally, woodland deer had to be made valuable, at least to the point where the revenue brought in would roughly balance an irreducible degree of damage. Venison marketing was gradually improved, so that an average of around 12.5p per lb in the early 1960s gradually rose to 75–120p per lb by the late 1980s. At this, venison represented a valuable asset if it was harvested at no cost to the estate. A crash in price in 1990, caused by political changes in Eastern Europe, was equally a disaster for deer welfare. The long-term effects cannot be assessed at present.

The post-war generation of woodland stalkers set out to deal with a pest, and had their sport for nothing. In many areas it is still low-cost sport, the province of enthusiasts who are keen enough to be out early and late, for woodland deer have learned long ago that dawn and dusk are the safest times to feed.

Britain was largely disregarded on the Continent as a trophy-producing country, and few people came from Europe to stalk. However, the British exhibit at the International Trophy Exhibition at Budapest, in 1972, produced a sensation, and since then there has been a keen demand for first-class roe stalking over here. This has allowed the employment of professional woodland stalkers and the development of sporting agencies catering for overseas and native stalkers. In addition, many gamekeepers include deer management in their duties. The revenue brought in by venison sales and letting stalking keeps many of them in employment at a time when the costs of running a game shoot have escalated. Prices for woodland stalking equate roughly to current rates for the open hill, perhaps £200 and upwards per day or per deer, except for certain very large red stags living in dense woodland which command much higher prices. The capital value of one harvestable Highland stag per annum has been put at £12,000 (late 1980s). The value of good roe stalking in the south cannot be far behind.

There is no objection on conservation grounds to the letting of stalking, provided that it does not lead to over-exploitation. It is true that many overseas visitors only want to take mature males, and this has to be rigidly limited to the sustainable yield. Their lack of local knowledge and the fact that they may have different sporting traditions at home make it essential that they are accompanied by a professional until he is satisfied of his client's safety and responsibility. If the visitor is only paying for the cream – the best trophies – then he must pay at the same time for the rest of the year's work – culling females and juvenile males – which can be offered at low cost to keen stalkers who are sufficiently dedicated and skilled to carry out a proper management plan.

Stalkers have been known to complain about the high prices asked for good roe stalking, but the 'red carpet' client can be reasonably expected to pay for his privilege and for his guide, while there is plenty to do for the rest of the year for the less well-funded. Other considerations apart, only roe and red deer are lettable in the main. Fallow, and more especially muntjac, offer opportunities for low-cost sport which are almost unexploited at the moment. Woodland stalking has the advantage that it is accessible without necessarily long journeys. Deer can be found in close proximity to large towns, though they are rarely noticed by the general public (until their roses are nipped off!). To be out in the woods as dawn breaks reveals a world which the urban majority can never imagine.

In contrast to open-hill stalking in Scotland, the woodland stalker creeps along the woodland paths, or waits in a likely position where the deer will drift his way on their way to or from the feeding grounds. If the ground is flat, he uses a shooting tower, or 'high seat' from which to observe and shoot safely. The direction of the wind is critical. Also, if the deer catch a whiff of human scent, the stalker is unlikely to see much. Their hearing, too, is tuned for the slightest untoward noise.

Stalking a rutting fallow buck in the autumn woods, with a camera as much as with a rifle, is most exciting.

Because deer numbers are high and the shooting pressure slight, the legal open seasons are long in comparison to other countries. In general, the males are hunted when they are in hard antler, and the does during the winter, after their young have become independent. It makes no difference to a male deer when he is shot, but selection is easier when he is carrying his antlers, which are indicators of good health and quality.

Greater ethical problems have to be faced when considering when to cull females. Often the criticism is raised that stalkers are shooting pregnant females. If the need to control females at all is agreed, then one can examine this question dispassionately. Is one's greater responsibility to the foetus, or the living fawn? There can be little doubt that to orphan a fawn before it is fully independent is cruel. At least the foetus dies with the mother. Therefore stalkers try to delay culling mature females until late enough in the winter to see last summer's offspring capable of survival. By that time inevitably there are visible signs of the next pregnancy. One hopes to complete the cull as soon as possible, but achieving it is paramount. Otherwise the deer will die anyway.

Muntjac are non-seasonal breeders and fawn every seven months. They mate again a few days after parturition, so they can be said to be continuously pregnant. This dilemma has to be squarely faced by every stalker. The pragmatic answer is that deer numbers can only be controlled by shooting females, and if we still had our large natural predators, they would not have our qualms, or wait for the most humane moment to take their breakfast. Nature is never kind.

Males of the large deer (red, fallow and sika) are in hard antler from late summer until the following spring, but stalkers try to achieve their cull before the rut when they are in their best condition, and to eliminate poor breeding stock before they mate. Roebucks clean their antlers in spring and shed them in the late autumn. Yearling bucks are still in velvet until May or early June. It is logical to pursue them in the summer, though their habit of feeding in the fields in April makes this month a good time to collect the necessary number of yearlings – to the satisfaction of their host, the farmer. Yearlings are then easily identified as such, and the fact that they are still in velvet means that there is less forest damage from fraying (rubbing off the velvet on young trees) than would otherwise be the case. The business of shooting young males may seem strange, but both with the object of reducing damage and harvesting the venison crop, this age class has to be trimmed severely. (The farmer does not, after all, wait until his lambs are three years old before sending them to market. He just keeps enough to maintain his breeding stock.)

STANDARDS FOR STALKERS

The British Deer Society, since its formation in the 1960s, has been seeking ways in which to improve the management and treatment of deer. An essential element in this is the performance of every individual stalker. Does he know enough to manage his deer properly? Can he shoot accurately? Does he know and obey the law? Is he making the best use of the deer he shoots? Above all, is he following the strictest rules of safety in the handling and use of his rifle? There is thus a duty to the deer, to the owner of the land, and to the public. We are a largely urban society without that intimate contact with country lore and values which was the regular background of the majority of shooters in the past. The elements have to be learned, and if enough deerstalkers are to be trained to cope with our massive deer population, this training has to be formalised, not merely passed on by personal precept and example (valuable though such instruction may be). In addition, the public, landowners, and not least the police, have to be convinced that stalkers are capable of demonstrating their suitability to be allowed to wander in our overcrowded land with a lethal weapon. There is confusion in the public and the official mind between careless handling and the actions of criminals or the insane, but the obligation remains.

Training courses have been run for many years by the British Deer Society, the British Field Sports Society, The Game Conservancy, the Forestry Commission and the British Association for Shooting and Conservation. A private organisation, the St Hubert Club, was the first to formalise its members' training into successive grades, with a test at each stage. This enterprise has now been followed up by the British Deer Society, which now offers a complete syllabus of lectures for courses at basic and advanced levels, which have also been adopted by the British Field Sports Society, Game Conservancy and BASC. Students having attended the course can sit for the appropriate competence certificate, which demands a certain level of knowledge and ability in deer identification and natural history, the law, marksmanship and the safe handling of firearms. The advanced level covers deer management, in addition to a higher level of ability in the other subjects. Since its launch in 1988, nearly 1,000 stalkers, or possibly twenty per cent of the total, now hold the National Stalker's Competence Certificate. One Agricultural College is already running a one-year Deer Management Course, and a syllabus at University level has been prepared, which only awaits the necessary funding.

A GREEN SPORT

Deerstalking is thus the easiest of sports to support on 'green', or conservation, grounds. It is widely recognised that the population has to be kept to a reasonable level, and that this can only be achieved humanely through the activities of well-trained stalkers using modern rifles of suitable calibre. The objects of management are fully consistent with the welfare of our deer herds in the context of a small island where multiple land use has to be accepted. Indeed, safeguarding the interests of farming and forestry is implicit in them. No government subsidies are demanded, no pollution or destruction of the environment is involved, and the only by-product is a supply of nutritious, low-fat, organically-grown meat.

Stalkers have a remarkably clean record for safe firearms handling, though this can never be a matter for complacency. A comprehensive scheme of training and re-training is available to all comers. In common with other sports, a revised and enlarged Code of Practice for deerstalkers is in preparation (the first was issued by the British Deer Society in 1970). Greed and incompetence are not unknown among stalkers, but it can be said that the great majority do their best for the deer they love, and the standard is steadily improving.

FALCONRY

Diana Durman-Walters

Diana Durman-Walters, a professionally trained teacher in falconry, has been involved in the sport for over twenty years. She is co-director with her husband, Leonard, of the Scottish Academy of Falconry and Related Studies, an institution recognised internationally for the results it achieves. The Scottish Academy is also proud of its kennel of German wirehaired pointers, an important adjunct to the hunt. She is chairman of the falconry committee of the British Field Sports Society's Scottish branch. The grouse-hawking moor over which Diana and Leonard Durman-Walters fly their peregrines is celebrated as one of the best for that pursuit in Scotland.

When falconry relied upon the taking of young from the wild in order to practice the sport, only a few privileged licence-holders were able to participate. This system could not absorb the growing number of aspirants; and, as those numbers swelled, so the need to perfect the art of captive breeding became a necessity. The major breakthrough in this field came in the early 1970s when the United States began to produce peregrine falcons in their project at Cornell University. The alteration of the birds' natural environment produced an almost catastrophic effect upon peregrines in the wild. However, by 1981, considerably more than 1000 peregrines had been bred in captivity and an equal number had been released into the wild.

Much of this work was done by falconers who made a close study of the breeding science. Falconers are, almost by definition, ardent conservationists, a fact shown in their instinctive understanding of the ecological value of their sport. Hawking (the generic term used to describe hunting) can only continue if the habitats are sufficiently abundant and of adequate variety to hold the quarry species. So far, in its 2000 year history, falconry has maintained an equilibrium between supplies of hawks and the management of land that is right for the quarry species.

At the turn of the last century, when the shotgun was the principal means of securing game for the pot, gamekeepers on shooting estates took the view that the only good bird of prey was a dead one. There was a relentless persecution in the attempt to annihilate raptors. But it remains uncertain as to whether all the killing and molestation during that period had any lasting

impact on the size and distribution of raptor populations. There are unfortunately still many people today who would like to do away with our
raptors altogether. But falconers have exercised great influence, particularly
where keepering is concerned. They have helped to make gamekeepers
aware of the need to preserve and maintain the breeding territories of hawks
and falcons. Much of this has been done through personal contacts, for
many falconers have access to estates during the game-hawking season.
Most keepers that I know now show a great affection for sport raptors, a fact
that I have particularly noticed when they have accompanied me on a hunt
and have seen at close quarters the skill of a trained bird and the relationship
between the bird and myself.

Landowners invited to a day's hawking are similarly impressed by all that
goes into falconry and are thus encouraged to preserve areas on their estates
in which suitable quarry species may breed and multiply. Many of our
ancestors would have been most fastidious in such endeavours. In medieval
times there was a high premium on well-trained raptors. If any man was
found guilty of stealing a hawk then the same would be done to him as if he
had stolen a horse. He would be hanged. Men of the church were much
addicted to the sport and lent their support in civil law. During the reign of
Edward III somebody stole a hawk from the Bishop of Ely, and the Bishop
excommunicated him, which by today's standards would be the equivalent
of the stigma of a prison sentence.

It was not so popular with Elizabeth I, but her successor, James I, was an
enthusiastic falconer. An act of his, passed in the first year of his reign,
forbade the use of guns, crossbows or longbows to kill game, making an
exception in favour of persons who kept hawks, thus placing very strong
proof of the importance of falconry in the early seventeenth century. The
Civil War caused a temporary demise in hunting and hawking. Many of
those who had enjoyed sport with hawk and hound were afterwards no
longer able to afford it. Improvements in the capacity of the sporting gun
then making shooting more popular, the halcyon days of falconry were over
for ever. Yet the Royal mews kept by George II – under Charles Beauclerk,
Duke of St Albans – still maintained a master falconer on a salary of £1,372
10s per annum and the office was not a sinecure. The king himself did not go
in for hawking, but his son, Frederick Prince of Wales, loved the sport. With
further improvements in firearms, coupled with the Enclosure Acts of
George III, however, it suffered another decline. When the old 'common
field' system of agriculture was the norm in most parts, when there were few
hedges and fences, hawks could be flown nearly everywhere. With the
advent of these obstructions (as the falconer would regard them) the conditions were so radically changed in favour of the quarry that the sport
became much more difficult. The hedge or wall were to afford the game
cover under which it could evade the stoop of the falcon and make good its

escape. Open country is the only country in which the long-winged hawk can be flown with any real chance of success. It was, for example, the conversion of the Yorkshire wolds into corn land that led the famous Colonel Thornton to leave his native county and migrate to Wiltshire, on whose downs he could continue his beloved sport. During his time much interest was shown in forming a club. In 1783 Colonel Thornton established, with the Earl of Orford, a club that had sixty members and owned thirty-two peregrines, thirteen goshawks and seven Iceland falcons.

It was not until after the Second World War that falconry really revived. Following the desperate need to grow crops for the hungry nation the need to eliminate crop failure from the ravages of predatory insects saw the introduction of pesticides, which soon proved highly toxic. The thinning of eggshells in the peregrine falcon at eyrie sites throughout Britain prompted

a major scientific field study. While this work was in progress falconers world-wide began to investigate the possibilities of breeding falcons and other raptors in captivity.

Falconers have always been at the forefront of endeavour when it has come to monitoring indigenous raptor populations. The early monarchs and their landowning subjects, condemning interference at eyrie sites, were thereby early conservationists, a virtue they held in common with those American falconer-scientists attempting to stem the decline of the anatum peregrine. Both were devoted to the campaign for the future survival of the species. Those devoted Americans were in no small way responsible for the effective control placed on the use of DDT in the northern hemisphere. In Britain, voluntary restraints on the use of this insecticide, urged by the hawking organisations, began earlier than in other countries, since when the peregrine has shown a marked increase in numbers, and these have now exceeded figures prior to the Second World War. But it was owing to breeding projects in the United States, Britain, West Germany and France that, in the late 1980s, the most encouraging results emerged. The world in general owes a great debt to scientists in the United States for their research into captive breeding of diurnal birds of prey. Once this knowledge was available falconers everywhere made good use of it. Breeding of raptors had previously been considered a hopeless cause, so difficult that it had been considered impossible to repopulate the wild. However, by the early 1980s, an impressive number of peregrines, gyrfalcons, sakers, lanners, prairie falcons, merlins and other species had been raised each year by an ever increasing number of establishments worldwide.

It is probable that all birds of prey species can now be bred in captivity, including eagles, which means that no species of raptor need become extinct. So falconers can produce their own birds for training and hunting; it is no longer necessary to take birds from the wild. The combined cost of the various programmes has amounted to several million pounds and has involved several thousand people. This is not to forget the support of governments, conservation bodies and trusts. It would be hard to find a parallel effort devoted to a single type of bird, throughout the story of conservation.

This major breakthrough has given rise to the growing numbers of falconers practising their sport – as many as in centuries past. Unfortunately, falconry attracts an unusual number of eccentrics, exhibitionists and extremists of one sort or another. These types, who are never skilled falconers, corrupt the sport for their own dubious ends, leaving a deplorable image with the general public who may thus have doubts about falconers in general. Inexperienced amateurs can join a falconry club or take a course at a school selected by them. There falconers are taught how to perfect the skills of husbandry, management and, of course, the control requisite for

flying, which, in turn, of course, develops the skill of the falcon. Those hawks belonging to amateurs who stay outside the scope of the clubs and their schools are unlikely to lead happy lives, as frequently too many mistakes are made, mistakes which could so easily be avoided. Responsible falconers recognise the problems besetting their sport. They acknowledge the need for effective regulations which protect the bona fide falconer from radical elements, as well as recognising the concern of the public for the conservation of birds of prey.

Falconry's history shows it to be one of the oldest of field sports. We think it is the most intellectually demanding and educational form of hunting ever practised, for it requires a high degree of skill and dedication. It arouses a deep appreciation of nature; it demands a practical study of natural history; and it very often leads to more useful scientific research. Detailed techniques and observations offer room for study that would otherwise be difficult to make. The ultimate expression of the sport comes in the handling and flying of the dynamic raptor. The strong bond that exists between man and hawk becomes most obvious when the hawk has gone out of sight in the chase and comes looking for her falconer; or, if she is fairly vocal, calls to him as soon as he (or she) is sighted. Nothing is more exciting to the falconer than the hawk's stoop as she singles out her quarry hundreds of feet below and, like a descending arrow, accelerates to her target. Below her, perhaps, a dog has been rigid on point, and, at the optimum height that the falcon could attain, her falconer urges the pointer forward to flush out the game. This perfect symbiosis between man and his environment heightens the senses and brings about a glorious feeling of natural harmony. As the falconer exhilarates in his hawk's supreme skills he should become fleetingly aware of his own limitations, yet tastes that moment of spontaneous union with the living world around him. Falconry has carried, in every age, a chivalrous, a spiritual and sometimes even a religious aura about it.

COURSING

Charles Blanning

Charles Blanning was brought up with racing and coursing greyhounds, his family having bred and trained them for over sixty years. He is the present Secretary of the National Coursing Club and also the Keeper of the Greyhound Stud Book, which registers all the pure-bred greyhounds in this country, both for coursing and track racing. He is the coursing correspondent of the *Racing Post*. He is also the co-author of *The Waterloo Cup* and *A Coursing Year*, and his definitive history of the greyhound and coursing will be published in 1991. Educated at King's School, Bruton, and at Christ's College, Cambridge, he worked variously as a schoolmaster and as director of a dairy product business before taking up his present position.

The true sportsman does not take out his dogs to destroy the hares, but for the sake of the course, and the contest between the dogs and the hares, and is glad if the hare escapes.

Those words were written 1800 years ago, but they sum up the coursing man's attitude to his sport today as accurately as they did in the time of their author, Flavius Arrianus, a Roman citizen writing in the second century AD. Coursing is often claimed to be the oldest of field sports, and there is no doubt that it was already popular in the ancient Egyptian and Persian civilisations, a recognisable greyhound type reaching Europe many centuries before Christ. It was the Romans, however, using 'celtic hounds' in competition to course brown hares, who ushered in a form of sport which has changed little in two thousand years. There is considerable evidence, in fact, that the brown hare, unlike the blue or mountain hare, is not indigenous to the British Isles and was imported by the Romans for sporting purposes.

Modern coursing, although popular in Elizabethan times when the first code of rules was drawn up, really started in 1776 when the first 'public' coursing club was founded by the third Earl of Orford at Swaffham in Norfolk. It is a measure of the continuity of tradition that the club still flourishes and the sport is staged over the same land at Westacre as it was two hundred years ago. The early clubs at Swaffham, Ashdown, Newmarket and Malton were confined to fewer than thirty members, all of them wealthy landowners.

As the popularity of sport increased in the 1850s, coursing, especially, was one that caught the imagination of the new rich. Huge meetings on the downs near Stonehenge or at Newmarket would attract between one and

two hundred runners, and would take a week to complete. Class was now
no barrier to entry. The meetings at Bothal in Northumberland and others in
the north east were dominated by dogs owned by pitmen. Along with horse
racing it became the spectator sport of the masses, daily crowds of sixty to
seventy thousand people attending the sport's premier meeting, the Waterloo Cup, at Great Altcar in Lancashire.

Coursing no longer commands the following of its Victorian heyday, but
there is still substantial support from a wide cross-section of country sports
followers. There are twenty-three greyhound coursing clubs affiliated to the
National Coursing Club, as well as several private greyhound meetings and
national clubs for other breeds such as whippets, deerhounds, salukis and
afghans. The Waterloo Cup, which can draw crowds of more than 7000
people (something of a miracle in the video age considering the bitter
weather found at Altcar in February), is a place of pilgrimage for sporting
all-sorts including lords, ladies and lurchermen, farm workers, famous
jockeys, 'Hooray Henrys', miners and Irish priests.

The National Coursing Club has administrated greyhound coursing since
its foundation in 1858. In 1882 it started its Greyhound Stud Book, which
became the model for the stud books of Ireland, the United States and
Australia, and today its Secretary still acts as the Keeper of the Stud Book
which registers all the pure-bred greyhounds in England, Scotland and
Wales, whether they run on the track or on the coursing field.

All the twenty-three clubs affiliated to the NCC have to run their meetings to its code of rules, a code so strict that it makes coursing the most tightly controlled field sport of all. Clubs for other breeds, such as whippets and deerhounds, also run as close to NCC rules as the unique qualities of their dogs allow. Opponents of coursing find it difficult to grasp that the very nature of the sport insists on the quarry having every chance to escape. As the purpose of coursing is to test the merits of two dogs only, it is essential that the hare be given every chance to evade the dogs, otherwise the whole object is negated. The rule which governs the 'slip', the releasing of the two dogs, illustrates most clearly that the objectives of coursing and its sporting nature are indivisible. The slip 'should not be less than eighty yards. The slipper shall not slip the dogs if, in his opinion, the hare is in a weak condition or balled up.' The length of the slip, which on suitable flat ground such as at Altcar, can be more like 120 yards, has two purposes; firstly, to provide the long run to the hare before she is turned for the first time which allows the pace of the dogs to be judged, and secondly, to give the hare every chance to outstay and outmanoeuvre the dogs.

There are strict regulations governing the fields coursed over. The grounds must not be enclosed, thus ensuring that the hare is given every chance to escape. On several coursing fields, special 'soughs' or artificial escapes are installed in which the hares can take refuge at the end of a course. At Altcar, where there has been coursing for over 160 years, there are numbers of soughs, the most famous example being the bank at the end of the 'Withins', the field where the first and last days of the Waterloo Cup are run. The end of the field is a maze of reeds, bridges and tunnels by which the hares can easily evade their pursuers. In the 1989–90 season at NCC meetings, six out of seven hares coursed escaped unharmed.

Coursing is probably the only field sport which takes positive steps to help the quarry escape. Coursing is the testing of two greyhounds or similar 'gazehounds' (running exclusively by sight) which are assessed by a complex system of points scoring. Its basis lies in the contrasting abilities of pursued and pursuer. The dogs may be faster but the hares are more agile and possess more stamina. The dog which has shown the superior speed and courage to be placed to make his quarry turn is rewarded by winning points awarded by a judge, who closely follows the course on horseback. Each dog wears a distinguishing red or white woollen collar, and at the end of the course the judge waves a handkerchief of the appropriate colour to show the winner; the dog which has scored the more points.

Greyhounds have been bred for centuries for speed, as the dog which shows the superior pace from slips to the first turn can be awarded a maximum of three points in addition to the one scored for turning the hare. For this reason the dog with the early turn of speed more often than not wins the course, for it takes a very brave dog to overturn such an advantage, or a very bad one to throw it away once it has been achieved. After the 'first turn' the dog which subsequently forces the hare to turn scores a single point, or a half point if the hare is turned at an angle of less than ninety degrees.

This points system makes nonsense, of course, of the widely-held belief that the dog which kills the hare wins the course. If this was the case, only one in seven courses would ever be decided. A single point only can be awarded for a kill, and then only if the dog does so by his own merit, not if he is aided by the other runner. In other words the kill can only decide the course if it is meritorious and if the dogs were previously level on points, a rare occurrence indeed. If, as they are frequently accused, coursing people took pleasure in seeing hares killed, the present rules of the sport would seem eccentric in the extreme. It is not difficult to kill hares with dogs if you wish to; you would simply let as many go as you could as close to the hare as possible.

The running of NCC coursing meetings is in the hands of the stewards appointed by the organising club, but there is another official in attendance appointed by the National Coursing Club itself. This is the Coursing Inspector whose duties are solely concerned with the hare. The Coursing Inspector has to ensure that the ground used for coursing gives the hare every chance of escape. If an unacceptable number of kills take place, the Coursing Inspector can insist on the coursing being stopped and the meeting stewards taking suitable action.

Opponents of coursing make much of the fact that the brown hare numbers are declining in this country. This decline has nothing to do with coursing and a great deal to do with modern farming methods. Indeed research by the Game Conservancy has proved conclusively that, on estates where coursing takes place, hare numbers are increasing against the national trend.

The halcyon period for the hare in Great Britain was the last century when both Victorian high farming and the enormous popularity of field sports encouraged the preservation of game on a massive scale. The four-course rotation of crops popular at the time provided the cover and forage essential to the hare throughout the farming year. Even so the contemporary reports of the hundreds of coursing meetings which took place all over the country always took care to thank the landowner for 'preserving' the hares for the coursing. What would have happened otherwise is obvious from the experience in Scotland after the Ground Game Act of 1880. The preservation of game and the consequent crop damage had been a sore point with tenant farmers for many years as the ground game was legally the property of the landowner; a committee had been set up to investigate grievances as early as 1846. In the 1870s, however, a period of serious agricultural depression, it became a parliamentary issue and in 1880 legislation, popularly known as the 'Hares & Rabbits Bill', was passed making the ground game the property

of the tenant. In Scotland in particular the farmers' guns exacted an orgy of revenge and the majority of the coursing meetings and the hares disappeared overnight, never to return.

The enemies of the brown hare in this century have been modern farming methods, foxes, poachers with lurchers and the shotgun. The prevailing system of monoculture in cereal-growing areas has left the hares without food and cover at vital times of the year in contrast to the varied plenty offered by Victorian crop rotation. The hares are most vulnerable after the harvest. With the landscape in September and early October as bare as the surface of the moon, the hares have virtually nothing to eat. Many people are puzzled by hares being picked up dead from coccidiosis and liver problems at a time when the weather is comparatively mild. The root cause of such deaths is starvation which leaves the hares weakened and vulnerable to disease. Sprays have often been blamed as a direct cause of hare deaths through poisoning, but in fact the eradication of the weeds on which hares can feed as a last resort proves even more lethal. In former times stubbles were allowed to stand in autumn and 'green up' before they were ploughed, affording both fodder and refuge for the hares. Now they are cultivated within days of the harvest.

The prevailing fashion for winter cereals will provide hares with good feeding throughout the winter as they relish the young shoots as soon as they are through, and it is only in the spring when cereal stalks become unpalatable that the forage search becomes critical again. Grass is a great standby for hares throughout the year, but, of course, it is a scarce commodity these days in arable country. It can be a mixed blessing where a grass economy predominates. Where economic pressures have dictated animal stocking densities, the pressure has increased for yet more cuts of silage. The modern mower can cut as close as Sweeney Todd and is lethal to young leverets. In the old days when winter feed consisted of hay, supplemented by roots and kale, hares abounded in some grass countries, such as that which staged the huge Border Union coursing meetings at Longtown in Cumberland.

Today it is only on estates where game is carefully preserved that the brown hare can multiply and increase. The Newmarket experience, where those with long memories reckon that there are hare numbers on coursing grounds now as great as in the 1920s and '30s, shows that where game shooting and coursing combine, the hare can flourish despite all the modern pressures on land which is intensively farmed. The carefully preserved covers which help the survival of an estate's pheasants and, in particular, partridges, also assist the survival of the hares. The keepering reduces the hares' most dangerous predator, the fox, to an acceptable level. (In Dorset, a county not celebrated for its hare numbers, The Game Conservancy has calculated that hares provide 15.6 per cent of the fox diet; 80 per cent of young hares are lost to predation.) Coursing on such an estate guarantees the hares' immunity to the draconian shoots which are used to this day for control purposes. Although 'bags' do not match that of Holkham on 19 December 1877 when 1215 hares were shot in a day, a modern hare shoot in East Anglia can claim in excess of 500, destroying fifty to seventy per cent of the hare population at a single stroke. The Game Conservancy estimate the effect of a day's coursing on a hare population as 'negligible'. With shoots of this kind combined with the pressures of modern farming, all too often the hare numbers are unable to recover.

If coursing was to be abolished because of the ignorance of its opponents, it would sever forever the last tenuous connection which makes the brown hare a welcome integer in an estate's game preservation. With coursing gone, the hare would become a second-class citizen in game management, accelerating a decline from which it would never be able to recover.

Any abolitionist who congratulated himself on destroying organised coursing, would do well to realise that no legislation would deter what is popularly known as 'illegal coursing', although why it is not just called 'poaching', I cannot imagine. After all, if someone takes pheasants or salmon, it is not called 'illegal shooting' or 'illegal fishing', but the media welcomes any opportunity to couple coursing with illegality. The bully boys with their cross-bred dogs, bulging satchels of betting money, and 4-track vehicles would continue to terrorise the countryside while the abolitionists were safe at home in Hampstead Garden Suburb, and the coursers, with their 2000-year tradition of fair play, had gone forever. There is no need for a judge, rules, or 'law' here. The dogs are slipped singly as soon as the hare gets up with no law given and the bets are decided, appropriately enough, like a 'sudden-death' play-off in golf. The first dog that fails to kill his hare loses.

The House of Lords Committee, which enquired into coursing in 1976, recommended legislation permitting coursing under certain rules and conditions, all of which mentioned in its report are now voluntarily observed by the National Coursing Club. The Committee's recommendation never came to anything, opponents of coursing preferring to try to destroy in ignorance rather than learn, consider, and construct. In the future coursing would have nothing to fear from such legislation and the countryside would have everything to gain.

FISHING

Sandy Mitchell

Sandy Mitchell was educated at Marlborough, where he regularly fished the stretch of the Kennet of which he had charge; then at St Edmund Hall, Oxford, from there proceeding to Lincoln's Inn to qualify as a barrister. For two years he worked in the corporate finance department of an international investment bank in the City of London, before turning to journalism. Now on the environmental side of *Country Life*, he is closely responsible for that magazine's field sports interests. He has fished in Ireland, New Zealand, Canada and Continental Europe as well as (extensively) in Britain. He is a dedicated wildlife conservationist.

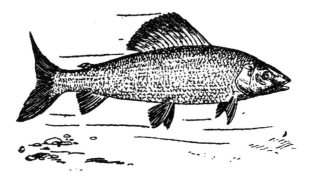

Fishing is probably the most contemplative, and is by any calculation the most popular of country sports. While waiting for a fish to bite, one has the hours for reflection that are denied to the galloping hunt-follower and the busily firing gun. And its popularity? The latest estimate suggests some four million people fish regularly in Britain: around one in fifteen of the nation's total population. With so many participating, the potential for causing suffering to the quarry and damage to fishing waters is obvious; with so much time to consider the consequences, fishermen have the least excuse for causing ill effects.

In the 1990s, one can sense that the majority of fishermen are aware of a duty to examine their sporting practices closely. Look at the passion that goes into the debate among coarse fishermen on the use of keepnets, or among trout anglers on the pros and cons of a catch-and-release fisheries policy. Yet, ask an honest fisherman why he worries about his use of barbed hooks or glutting his pond with stocked fish, then wait a while for the reply: 'On the one hand, there is self-interest. What is good for the fish is good for the fisherman. On the other, I want to fish in a sporting manner.'

This chapter is informed by the belief that it is no longer enough for fishermen simply to consult their own self-interest and grab for that slippery touchstone, fair play, when trying to define good practice. Fishing cannot expect to remain hidden forever from the public scrutiny that its fellow country sports have undergone. Nor, as pressure on the countryside increases, should fishermen enjoy exclusive access to their waters, unless they can show they are the best possible custodians of rivers, lakes and ponds. So, to sustain their sport, fishermen must consider both the common perception of their activities, and the environmental effects.

It can fairly be objected at the outset that, if the 'green' fisherman's concern is solely with bettering the lot of fish, the best thing he can do is to give up fishing altogether. This is certainly the view of the Campaign for the Abolition of Angling, who believe that fish have rights just as humans do. They say that there is no possible justification for wilfully causing pain, even if it is the lowliest eel that may be suffering.

Against this, some fishermen would argue that there is no need to worry about the issue of cruelty, because fish simply cannot feel a hook in their mouths, or even one that is swallowed as far as the stomach. Would a pike eat a spiny stickleback, or a soft-lipped grayling a prickly shrimp, if they could feel what they had in their mouths, they ask. And, surely – so this argument runs – if a fish were hurt by a hook, it would not rush away from the fishermen as fish generally do when hooked, but would try to lessen the pain by swimming towards the rod.

But this defence to the Campaign's contention is not convincing, and if widely accepted by fishermen would do the sport great harm. Fish may easily be duped into taking a bait at one time, but – as fishermen often have cause to regret – at another the slightest touch of a hook will make them spit it out. This is why one needs to strike with lightning speed when, for example, a trout rises to a fly. It takes great imagination to separate that degree of sensitivity from any ability to feel pain. And as for a fish swimming in the direction of the line's pull, one can object that, if a fish does feel pain it is still most likely to grit its teeth and pull away, so that it might escape with its life.

Nor will the most unbiased scientific opinion come to the fisherman's rescue on this point. Even some fifteen years ago, when a panel of biologists and veterinary surgeons examined the issue, it was accepted that fish suffered pain. In the words of the Medway report: 'The evidence suggests that all vertebrates (including fish), through the mediation of similar neuro-pharmacological processes, experience similar sensations to a greater or a lesser degree in response to noxious stimuli.'* Even the lowliest eel.

So, fishermen must accept that their enjoyment involves the infliction of pain. With that acceptance comes a duty to minimise the potential hurt. Even in the unlikely event that one day it is conclusively proved that fish positively enjoy sucking on a sharp piece of metal, it can never be denied that catching fish often permanently damages them. Fish can be hooked in the eye, or hooked so that the mouth or gills tear. However fish are handled, they inevitably lose some of their protective slimy coating when they come to the bank. For anglers, there is no escaping a duty to the quarry.

As important as any subjective evidence of fish sensitivity is the impression that playing a fish makes on the uninformed, but concerned observer. 'Poor thing,' that person is bound to say as the fish writhes on the hook. It is to that person – perhaps tomorrow's voter for the sport's reform or abolition

* Report of the Panel of Enquiry into Shooting and Angling (1976–1979). Published by the RSPCA (1980) Chairman: Lord Medway.

– that the fisherman must justify his action, while perhaps half agreeing that what he does may be cruel.

Looking for philosophical support at this point, a fisherman could do worse than read the clear analysis of fishing ethics contained in a book called *Fishing and Thinking* (first published in 1959), by A. A. Luce, a professor of moral philosophy at Trinity College, Dublin. 'The defence and justification [of game fishing] are simply that the angler is killing fish for food,' it says there. But where does that leave the trout purist who has sworn to return every fish to the stream in order to preserve its stock of wild fish, or the match fisherman who would never dream of killing a prize carp?

The answer is that they are both in a highly vulnerable position. They can only try to persuade the onlooker that they have taken all possible steps to minimise the quarry's suffering, and that the benefits of fishing – as a healthy, popular recreation, and as a means of positive management of a natural resource – outweigh the remaining concern about the fishes' welfare.

But take a look at your local tackle dealer's. Is there anything in the shop that would persuade our concerned non-fishing friend that fish or environmental welfare is even at the back of fishermen's minds? The only flies, spinners or lures on sale in the shop will have barbed hooks. And, while advice on how to maximise your catch will come freely, no interest will be shown in how you dispose of the fish or in your treatment of the water.

'That would be rude and intrusive,' the dealers will object. 'If we don't treat our customers as responsible adults, they won't return. Besides, a fisherman's practices are a matter for his own conscience.' But the truth is that it would be neither rude nor intrusive to promote the sale of barbless hooks, for example, by explaining the disadvantages of using the barbed variety. It would be a kindness to explain to a novice angler how to unhook a fish (by holding it firmly in the water with wetted hands, and using a hook disgorger) or kill one cleanly (with a sharp blow on top of the head, directly behind the eyes).

Even if tackle-shop owners cannot bring themselves to advise their clients on the wider fishing issues, they should distribute copies of advisory literature. *The Game Angling Code*, produced in mid-1990 by a group of game-fishing bodies, is a handy booklet which suggests a set of principles for good fishing practice. The National Anglers Council has produced an equivalent for coarse fishermen. The National Federation of Anglers' *Nylon and Litter Code* and *Keepnet Code* also make informative reading.

Would it be going too far for the tackle shop to disseminate advisory literature from the RSPCA on fishing? That body, after all, is one of the most responsible animal-welfare bodies in Britain, and its membership is immense. Its views on fishing are based on the recommendations of the Medway report, and are therefore extremely well thought out. It is in fishermen's own interests to be aware of informed criticism, and to adapt their practice in its light.

And surely, it is for the owners of tackle shops to take all this trouble, to carry out what is in effect an 'environmental audit' of their business. They have as great an interest in ensuring the health of the sport as anyone. Moreover, by promoting fishing, they must assume some responsibility for how it is enjoyed.

If there is little excuse for dealers failing to consider what is done with all the hardware they sell, the blame is, at least, not wholly theirs. The vast majority of tackle manufacturers make it difficult for the supplier to stock products that do the minimum damage. Most manufacturers do not make flies, lures or baits using barbless hooks. Any packeted spinners, or plugs, come with at least one barbed point, and often a double or treble. The superior hooking characteristics are advertised on the packaging, but there is, of course, no mention of the problems the fisherman will face when unhooking a fish that he wants to return because it is, say, undersized.

A similarly irresponsible attitude is shown by manufacturers of nylon lines. Millions of spools are produced and sold each year. The makers compete in claiming their line is more invisible to fish than any other. Yet there is no word that it might also be invisible to animals and birds on the riverbank, and no caution that the line should be safely disposed of.

Not much effort would be required of manufacturers to change their image. A warning printed on the face of a spool of line would be a start. The next sensible step would be to fund research into bio-degradable lines. If sold with the 'sell-by date', in the manner of a pint of milk, the risk to the fisherman of breakage, from deteriorating line, could be avoided. And the more far-sighted companies might consider publishing information, to be enclosed with each of their items of tackle, on the environmental effects of their manufacturing processes. If such steps were taken, momentum towards responsible attitudes within the industry and on the riverbank would inevitably build up.

It is impossible to believe that a profit can't be turned from making such products that could fairly be labelled 'environmentally sensitive'. One has only to look at the investment being made by the supermarkets in marketing 'green' produce, to see the direction of consumer spending. And if the general consumer is quickly becoming more sensitive to these issues, how long will it take fishermen – who daily see the effects of pollution on their waters – to show concern at their support for a tackle industry which processes plastics and metals in great quantity.

If manufacturers need any further encouragement, they only have to recall what happened when the press, then Parliament, were alerted to the suffering caused to swans by coarse fishermen's lead weights to see how quickly the recklessness of the fishing industry can backfire.

Having pointed an accusatory finger at his suppliers, the fisherman must now open his own tackle bag to scrutiny. Two items should immediately be obvious: a hook disgorger, and a 'priest' for killing fish cleanly. These should both be sufficiently solid to cope with the size of fish that might be encountered.

Going prepared for every eventuality goes against the grain for many fishermen. In popular belief, the most sporting way to fish is to face nature on level terms, and eschew the advantages of available gadgetry. A couple of spinners or lures tucked into your capband are thought to be sufficient. Yet, a disgorger and priest would add little weight, and could save much distress.

What a fisherman takes with him on an outing, naturally leads onto how he fishes. And the idea of taking the minimum, frequently goes hand-in-hand with fishing 'fine and far off'. That is to say, using the lightest tackle possible to cope with the expected size of fish, and thereby giving the fish the best chance of fighting free of the hook's hold.

This style of fishing has a potent appeal for the sporting mind. But, here, traditional sportsmanship and sound environmental practice clash. A light line and rod certainly mean a testing fight for the fisherman, who has to persuade the fish away from sunken roots or weed and steer it to the bank, using only the gentlest pressure. For the fish, the fight ends either with breaking the line or with total exhaustion. The first alternative means the fish is left with a hook and line trailing from its jaw; anyone who has seen a fish frantically trying to rub against a root, so as to ease out the hook, knows just how the fish must find it.

The second possible outcome is no better. Having fought almost to its

death, the quarry has suffered the greatest stress and, presumably, pain. In addition, its exhausted condition means that its chances of survival if it is returned to the water are slim. Clearly, 'fine and far off' is least appropriate on a catch-and-release water. Yet on such waters, where there is evident concern for the stock, fishermen most commonly aspire to the highest degree of 'sportsmanship.'

The Medway report suggests guidelines for acceptable line breaking-strain. The general rule is to use a line that will be strong enough to play the largest type of fish you might catch on a particular water. An idea of what is appropriate can be gained from the recommendation that, for carp or barbel, an absolute minimum of 8lb breaking strain should be used, and for upland river fly-fishing, 6lb is the lightest.

This is a considerably heavier line than one might think suitable. And it may be objected that on a hot summer's day, the glassy surface of a lake or stream makes the lightest line stand out like a hawser. But, as with the use of barbless hooks, the price of keeping 'green' principles in mind may be fewer fish brought to the bank. On the other side of this equation is the fact that a fish caught on tackle suggested here as appropriate, is one caught against the odds. That, after all, is the claim made for the satisfaction in fishing fine and far off. (The National Federation of Anglers have specific advice for bait fishermen on line strengths: always use a paternoster or leger link of a lower breaking strain than the reel line, so that minimum line is lost in the event of breakage.)

Fishermen should also bear in mind that choosing a sturdy enough nylon leader is, on its own, not adequate to bring a fish quickly under control. A rod of the correct stiffness and length, and sufficiently strong hooks are also needed. Here again, the tackle dealer has a part to play in offering responsible advice.

Keepnets, as mentioned earlier, are already a source of heart-searching among fishermen. While the ideal would be to do away with them altogether, there seems little alternative to using them for match coarse-fishing. In the course of a competition a fisherman might catch as many as twenty or thirty fish, so it would be impractical for a judge to try to weigh and return each fish as it is caught. Good practice demands that fishermen use the most recently developed knotless-mesh nets, and ones with a remote-release mechanism that enables the bottom end of the net to open without removing the net from the water. (The *Keepnet Code* shows how to stake a net correctly.)

Match trout-fishing, far more than its coarse counterpart, must trouble the 'green' conscience. Each competitor may kill as many as eight trout in a day, and the motive for killing is simply to beat the next man's catch. How can that be differentiated from the long-banned sport of shooting live pigeons in competition?

Killing edible fish should always give fishermen pause for thought. It is hard to imagine that a paying rod ever needs to kill a fish for food, and impossible to believe that a regular fisherman can usefully dispose of a haul of half a dozen trout – the size of catch often set as a bag limit. Fish are often killed because the limit imposed by the rules of a fishery is taken as a target for which to aim. This creates a vicious circle. The fisheries manager thinks that to keep his customers he must continue with a heavy stocking policy. And because there are so many fish in the water, the fisherman believes he has failed if he does not catch his limit. The killing of a fish is reduced, as in competitive fishing, to a matter of simple addition. The quality of the fishing also suffers, as the speed of stock turnover is too fast to allow the fish to become naturally canny.

This cycle can be broken – or better, avoided completely – if fishermen discipline themselves to keep, at most, a single fish per day. More can be released without significant harm if balanced tackle and barbless hooks are used. Research has shown that the survival rate among carefully returned fish is as high as ninety per cent.

The final plea for fishermen to examine their own practice concerns fish livebaits. Their use among pike, perch and zander fishermen may be confined to a small minority. Yet, even if perpetrated by only a few, the cruelty of skewering fish on livebait mounts will do immense harm to the sport's image. (For an indicative reaction, just ask a trout fisherman how he feels about the sale by some reservoir fisheries of young trout as pike bait.) Direct harm can also be caused to fishing waters by non-native livebait fish that swim free of the mount. By this means disease is spread and the natural balance of fish species within a particular water is altered.

By this stage, it will be clear that many of the demands of 'green fishing' can affect the chances of catching fish. Some would say it is unrealistic to expect fishermen to accept the slightest lowering of their rate of success. Indeed, this might be so if fishermen were not supported by a mass of vigorous clubs, societies and associations. These bodies have even greater influence on fishing customs than the tackle trade, for they formulate the rules for particular waters, and so can lead opinion. They must encourage their subscribers to adopt the best practices.

One other factor must be brought into account as soon as one mentions any change that might affect the number of fish caught, and that is the commercial interests of fisheries owners. The price of a rod in a syndicate, a day ticket, and a fishing timeshare are all calculated with regard to the number of fish one can expect to catch, bearing in mind previous records. Fishing rights are coming increasingly to resemble tradeable commodities, like stocks and shares; and the trend will continue as the resource is put under ever-greater rod and environmental pressure. On their own, those with commercial fisheries interests will not welcome any practice that would

lower the index by which fishing value is judged. But just as tackle might command a premium for being environmentally friendly, so might fishing that is managed with sensitivity to the environment.

So far, my spotlight has been focused on the relationship between the angler and his immediate quarry. Just as significant, however, are the effects of fishing on waters as a whole. If a fisherman is fortunate enough to own the rights to a stretch of water, he is responsible for the management, and thus the condition, of his fishery. The same applies to the members of a syndicate or a club. Even a day-ticket holder can make his voice heard in the policy-making of the fishery, if he insists on telling the manager of his impressions, or writes them in the record book at the waterside.

For the environmentalist, fishery management is the area with the greatest room for positive effort and results. An immense variety of flora and fauna thrive close to or in clean water. Yet very few fisheries managers think beyond the welfare of their fish stocks.

The danger lurking behind the introduction of non-indigenous fish is of particular concern on trout waters. Our native wild trout strains are becoming endangered. Name any of the major Southern chalkstreams, and see how little of the native stock survives among the outsized rainbows and farm-bred browns. Fishermen have become their own worst enemies. They have succeeded in destroying the best of their sport, for a wild fish is infinitely superior to a stocked one: its fins will be better formed, its body better proportioned and the colouring of its skin will vary from speckled silver, through polka-dot green to black-flecked brown. Stocked trout tend to be uniform in colouring, and on the hook they seldom show the fierce spirit of the native.

When a water is stocked with non-native fish, the resident population suffers for two reasons. First, competition for available food is increased, and if the new fish are larger than the natives (generally the reason for stocking), they will win the best lies and, thus, the best food sources. Second, introduced brown trout will tend to breed with the native strains, thereby diluting the latter's genetic integrity. The native strain's characteristics, developed over thousands of years' adaptation to its particular environment, will be lost. Diversity becomes uniformity. The fisherman catches the same fish wherever he goes.

Before stocking, the fishery management should, therefore, ask itself if stocking is really necessary. Rather than pour in tame stockies, would it not be better to limit the number of rod visits and enjoy the testing sport provided by the wild half-pounders? If stocking is necessary, then the management must consider how stockies can best be prevented from escaping into connected river systems. Is a local strain of fish available from the supplying farm? Best of all is for local fisheries to pool their resources and fund a breeding programme for the native strain.

The real test of environmentally-sound fishery management, however, has little to do with the fish. It lies in the diversity of wildlife and plantlife to be found around the fishery. A fishery manager interested only in his stock is liable to reduce his water to a selfish monoculture. Sadly, the sight of banks mown like a lawn to ease the fisherman's access and casting is a common one. It would be easier and cheaper to allow bankside plants to flourish, bringing with them a place for grubs, butterflies and small birds. Habitat for moorhens, toads, newts or beetles can be provided simply by leaving undisturbed areas of scrub, hedge or fallen trees around the fishery. The pleasure of spending a day at the waterside, and the economic value of the resource are, surely, vastly increased by the presence of rich wildlife.

Practical, day-to-day conservation of fishing waters depends on techniques that have been used by keepers for generations. Waterkeeping is a subject that would fill a series of books – there is stocking, culling, lake or river-bed landscaping to consider, among other topics – but some inkling of its complexity can be gleaned from how keepers cope with water needs.

In the summer months, weed takes over the surface of many lakes and rivers. If it is not raked off or scythed back, the oxygen content of the water is liable to drop and the world beneath the water surface becomes gloomy and stagnant. A certain amount of weed is, nonetheless, essential as a home for fish and insects. And on rivers suffering from drought, weedbeds play a crucial role in maintaining river levels by slowing the rate at which the water disappears downstream.

In the winter, a great deal of water-plantlife dies, decomposes and forms a sediment on river or lake beds. Patches of clean gravel used by many fish for spawning, and by numerous insect species as a harbour for their eggs and growing young, can become clogged with a suffocating, fine silt. Active management demands that such silt is regularly raked away, removed by redirected water flow, or dredged off.

Clearly, effective weed management is an aspect of conservation that calls for intimate knowledge of the water concerned. Few fishermen, however, manage to visit the waterside as frequently as those who are fortunate enough to act as keepers. Yet all fishermen have a part to play in the conservation of their waters, and not only in making up for others' careless littering. The National Rivers Authority is happy to acknowledge that, often, the first warning they receive of a pollution incident comes from fishermen who have noticed a shoal of dead fish. In such instances, it is vital for the fisherman to report quickly the precise location of the fish kill and time the signs were spotted. Less dramatic indicators of pollution such as unusual discoloration or smell may imply an illegal factory discharge or leaking storage tank. A timely report to a fisheries officer can prevent serious harm, or at least a repetition of the incident.

No one can doubt that many coarse and game fisheries owe their continued existence to the sport, nor that the interest shown by the general public (and reflected in the news media) in the condition of our waters are largely owed to the influence of recreational anglers. Enthusiasts for the sport may also take pride in the fact that fishermen have long been in the forefront of the campaign against the careless exploitation and abuse of Britain's freshwaters, whether by farmers, industry or urban development.

Yet, where the numbers of fishermen are greatest – in densely populated areas – a fishery's management will undergo the sternest test of its green credentials. In such areas, it is common for both access to rivers and streams, and the water in them, to be the subject of extreme competition. Almost the entire length of many rivers, and circumference of many lakes, in the South of England is in private hands, and fishing on them is guarded jealously. The result is that the public is completely excluded from the banks, and can only glimpse the rivers from public bridges and the lakes through gaps in surrounding fences.

It is also the case in such highly developed areas as the South of England, that pure water is widely pumped from streams and rivers in order to supply local houses, farms and businesses. In dry summers – such as those of 1989 and '90 – local riparian owners and fishermen have demanded that abstraction is reduced, and that hose-pipe bans are introduced. But why, one has to ask, should all the local gardeners sacrifice their plants, the farmers their crops, and businesses their profits for the sake of the fish in a river they are never allowed to enjoy.

Suggest to the owner of a fishery that he might gain more support for his call for water rationing or the revocation of abstraction licences if he encouraged controlled access to his river, and his face will turn pale. 'I would rather fight alone than allow the public onto the riverbank,' he will say, fearing that his riverside peace will disappear and poaching will become a plague. But if a limited area of riverbank were set aside as a nature reserve for the public to enjoy, there need be nothing to fear. The code of behaviour in such reserves is well understood by the public. Appreciation of riverine life would be broadened as a result, and the fishing lobby would gain a wider audience.

Changing the priorities of a fishery in this way is a difficult step to take. However, if the fishery manager needs expert advice and support, he can look to the National Rivers Authority. The Authority – part Government, part self-funded – calls itself 'the strongest environmental watchdog in Europe'. Its statutory duties involve supervising the welfare and use of freshwaters. This specifically includes the duty to 'protect, maintain and enhance' fisheries.

The Authority's role requires it to balance the demands of the various recreational uses of freshwaters against the need for environmental conservation and public water supply. Therefore, the Authority applauds fisheries which open themselves to wider public access and show interest in the improvement of waterside habitats. Material help is readily provided by the NRA to such fisheries, and scientific guidance is given as freely. Just how much fishermen stand to benefit from the activities of the Authority is illustrated by events on the River Tees which flows into the sea at Stockton. As a part of an urban development programme, a large barrage is to be built across the estuary. This will have the effect of partially damming the river. The Authority is making sure that the stillwater formed by the dam will be of maximum benefit to wildlife and to local coarse fishermen. At the local NRA headquarters it is hoped that this area will become one of the best fisheries in the North of England. At the same time, the Authority is running a salmon re-introduction programme on the Tees, which involves strenuous efforts to reduce estuarine pollution together with large-scale hatching and stocking of parr. In five to ten years, salmon may be running the river in their thousands.

The fact that the NRA is also empowered to vary or revoke water-abstraction licences means that it is in the interest of fisheries to maintain good relations with the Authority. Every fishery manager should meet the local fisheries officer, invite him to the fishery, explain his own priorities and discover those of the NRA. The significance of this liaison was demonstrated on the River Test in Hampshire towards the end of 1990.

Local fishermen and riparian owners were worried by the condition of the river during the hot summer. Many thought the level was low, the flow slack and the water unusually murky, and this on the finest chalkstream in Britain! The NRA responded to this concern by convening a public meeting, which was attended by the body's chairman, Lord Crickhowell. At the meeting, it was pointed out by the authority's scientists that, judged by scientific criteria, the river had been in prime condition throughout the season. But, having listened to the representations of the fishing lobby at the meeting, the authority accepted that the quality of fishing on the river was of prime importance and that the necessary resources should be devoted to maintain that quality.

If the fishing lobby does not unite in the manner of that on the Test and does not seek liaison with the NRA, fishermen have themselves to blame for the results. What can happen is demonstrated by the small River Meon, which also runs through Hampshire. Having suffered similarly from a hot, dry summer in 1990, the river offered very poor fishing for most of the season. But only isolated calls for help and understanding were made to the NRA, which inevitably tailored its reaction to the force of the call made upon it. Thus, fishermen on the Meon have none of the satisfaction of knowing that in future years their interests are a priority for the authority.

This comparison illustrates the fact that it is a duty for fishermen to support and lobby sympathetic bodies. By his effect on improving the freshwater environment – directly, and indirectly via the NRA, for example – so the 'green' fisherman is judged.

It may now seem as though one needs the conscience of a moral philosopher, the energy of a political revolutionary and the benevolence of St Francis, to be an environment friendly fisherman; which, for most of us, would mean giving up the simple, untroubled pastime that is fishing. As for me, I would do nothing to spoil my greatest pleasure, and conclude that all that is required of fishermen is to keep in mind the virtues that Izaak Walton, in his *Compleat Angler*, attributed to the fish themselves: '. . . it is a loving and innocent fish that hurts nothing that hath life, and is at peace with all the numerous inhabitants of that vast watery element.'

SALMON FISHING

Crawford Little

After education at a naval cadet college, followed by the Royal Agricultural College, Cirencester, Crawford Little followed a career in estate management. He then started up a small publishing company, from which he launched the magazine *Countrysport*. Fishing and the conservation of game fish have always been his main interests. He landed his first fish, aged three, and at seven was casting with a fly. He has written four books on salmon fishing and is a regular contributor to the leading periodical on the subject, *Trout and Salmon*. He is also a keen game shot and was at one time vice-president of the Solway Wildfowlers Association.

What sort of salmon fishing will there be for our children and grandchildren? Some would offer a pessimistic answer. There are those who might go so far as to suggest that, in fifty years time, the wild species could be all but extinct, with sportsmen dependent upon closely guarded stillwaters stocked with the products of the local salmon farms.

It certainly cannot be denied that many rivers that enjoyed runs of salmon since the dawn of time fell out of production as a result of the industrialisation of so much of Britain and Continental Europe. In an ever increasing chase for profits the salmon, together with so many species, was subjected to political indifference. Angling interests who sought to protect the salmon have always been frustrated by inadequate legislation.

Many calls are placed upon our water resources and judgements made in arriving at a balance between the needs of the salmon for plentiful supplies of clean water and easy access, and those of the urban industrial sprawls for water and power supplies. Equally, it cannot be denied that with ever-increasing leisure time, it is possible to argue that there are simply too many fishermen chasing too few fish and that, in an age of sporting entrepreneurs putting up large amounts of money, some rivers have been subjected to unscrupulous methods in the search to increase catches and maximise capital and rental valuations. The list goes on. As stated, it would be tempting to forecast a bleak if not impossible future for the salmon and salmon rivers.

This would, however, deny the other side to the coin. And it is this opposite side that makes so many of us cautiously optimistic. For example, my boyhood memories hold a picture of two salmon swimming up the River Wear past the shipyards in Sunderland. They were steering into an obscene flow of raw, human sewage. Their chances of survival were slim at best. Yet today the Wear has been cleaned up, and it regularly produces catches of salmon. High in its tributaries, future generations of salmon are emerging in the ritual of spawning time, just as they were in centuries past. And who, twenty-five years ago would, even in their wildest dreams, have believed they could one day stand on a bridge in Newcastle and, looking down upon the desecrated water of the Tyne, see it regain its place as one of the most productive salmon rivers in England and Wales?

These and other success stories have shown that the protection and enhancement of salmon seems to be a simple concept. It requires little more than ensuring that rivers are fit places for salmon to spend their early years and then, certainly from the angler's point of view, to reduce and control, or eliminate, alternative forms of predation, harvest or other pre-spawning mortality. It *would* be simple if salmon could be treated like trout in a pond or pheasants on a shoot.

The problem with salmon conservation is, very largely, that they do not stay put. We can look to their needs as much as possible for the first few years of their life, but then they go off to sea, journeying to the rich feeding grounds of the North Atlantic and, until they return to the river as mature, ripe spawners, they may be literally thousands of miles away from our protection.

The conservation of the salmon, or any wild, migratory species, requires local effort, to be sure, but it needs a great deal more besides. Even a national determination to conserve salmon stocks is not enough. The salmon can only be protected through international agreements and, as such, must be viewed as dependent upon, and only a minor part of, a much greater concern for the planet and the species that inhabit it. Salmon anglers would be foolish if they did not recognise the level of this dependence and made the mistake of adopting an isolationist stance.

In their efforts to help shape social attitudes and political priorities, sportsmen must accept that their activities with the rod, as well as the rifle and gun, are not smiled upon in all quarters. However, the outpourings of a small but vocal band of tunnel-visioned 'greens' should not blind anglers to the fact that respected and thinking conservationists around the world accept that, where a wild species is managed to produce a surplus, it is not wrong to harvest that surplus. And all the better when that harvest is seen to create the interest and income to provide the required investment to protect and improve the species in its natural environment. Recognising this fact, more and more salmon fishermen have come to accept that they should not only want, but also need, to think in broad conservationist terms.

One part of this acceptance is the recognition that we might come into disagreement with the conservation movement in its widest sense in deciding who gets what share of the salmon surplus. Man is not the only reaper of the harvest and while we may have logic on our side in arguing for the control of certain fish-predators, be they mergansers gorging themselves on immature fish, or seals feasting on mature fish returning to the rivers, we should recognise that these species are emotive subjects as well as accepting that public opinion is likely to insist that wild, natural predators must be given the first bite of the cherry. Suggestions to the contrary are hardly likely to meet with approval and could lead to a loss of public and political support.

While we cannot talk in terms of exactitudes, the conservation of salmon must involve leaving sufficient stocks to continue the cycle, and hopefully to increase the species with a surplus to be taken by wild, predatory species; and, finally, for man to have a slice of the cake as a reward for his efforts. In regard to man's slice, it has to be then decided what portion should be given over to purely commercial interests and what this will leave for sport with rod-and-line. Traditionally, the netting companies tend to have held the whip-hand. Politicians and bureaucrats are naturally concerned to be seen to support industries and providers of employment in what are often remote rural areas.

Today, however, due to initiatives from the angling interests, and some long overdue surveys and reports, it has been clearly revealed that – in an age of increasing demand for sport and recreation – it is sport fishing that has been far and away the more important industry, and a massive creator too, of wealth, foreign income, and both direct and indirect employment. A salmon taken on rod-and-line may indeed be worth seventy times as much to the economy as the same fish taken in a net. The growth in salmon farming, while creating its fair share of problems, has been equally instrumental in sounding the death knell of a purely commercial harvest of wild salmon stocks.

Anglers have long held the view that netting should be eliminated

through natural redundancy, or by offering netsmen alternative employment in hatchery work, river improvement and protection and so on.
Recently very substantial sums of money have been raised in order to buy
out netting stations. At one level, this might be seen as little more than a
dog-in-a-manger attitude. It could be said that anglers simply want more
salmon swimming up their rivers in order that they can catch more of them
for themselves.

At this level it is true and, of course, perfectly understandable. However,
the problem goes deeper. Anglers feel a deep-seated revulsion at what they
see as the indiscriminate slaughter of a species that they love and respect. By
comparison to the efficiency of nets, anglers' efforts are seen to be woefully
ineffective. But, with angling, more salmon are left free to continue their
journey to the spawning redds. It could therefore be fairly said that salmon
fishing with rod-and-line produces maximum interest, income and investment in ensuring a bright future for the species, while having a minimum
effect on population levels. Many anglers are prepared to limit themselves to
fishing only with the fly and this is just one more manifestation of the
anglers' respect for the species, and championing the ethos that there is so
much more to salmon fishing than catching salmon.

Salmon anglers have taken, and must continue to take, a positive, vigilant
approach in ensuring that the salmon's special needs are recognised and
respected. There will be times when salmon-anglers will feel, as they have
done in the past, that they stand alone in seeking to protect the wet, slimy
and normally invisible, in a world where the television-viewing public are
more tuned in to the seemingly cuddly, warm and high-profile species.
However, by convincing the decision-makers that salmon are worth greater
consideration in the scheme of things – in their own right as well as a symbol
of pure water – and that angling is the most logical and acceptable means,
not only of harvesting the surplus but also of ensuring the best possible
environment for this noble fish, then the future should be well assured.

In the meantime, at national and local levels, angling interests will undoubtedly continue in their role as virtually the only champions of the fish
for its own sake. They will carry on with the struggle to ensure that the
salmon's needs are made known to the decision-makers. Who else will cry
out when a river's entire stock of salmon and sea trout are literally extermi-
nated overnight by a deluge of acid rain? Who else even among the 'greens',
would even note their passing? Who else will argue so strongly to maintain
stability in our rivers – the stability of the river beds and banks, as well as the
water flow upon which so much of the nation's flora and fauna depends?
Salmon anglers and their representative bodies continue to hold a watching
brief on both water resource and associated land developments. Included in
that brief are land and hill drainage for both agriculture and forestry;
ploughing and planting; water and gravel extraction; the effects of fish

farming and hatcheries; predators, and netting and poaching by highly organised and ruthless gangs. These are all activities that might swing the balance in the salmon's fight for survival into the next century. There is really no one but the salmon angler to protect the salmon's interests.

Wider conservation interests and an environmentally aware society are providing us with cleaner rivers and restoring some sort of balance. Government cannot drag its heels over such matters as acid rain for very much longer. It will be left to the anglers alone to ensure that the rivers, estuaries, coasts and high seas are managed at least with respect for the needs, benefit and productivity of the migratory salmon. There is no doubt that the depth of feeling and the determination of salmon-anglers and the rod-and-line industry is greater than ever before.

ASSOCIATIONS

**Association of Masters of Harriers
and Beagles**
J. J. Kirkpatrick
Horn Park
Beaminster, Dorset DT8 3HB
Tel. 0308 862212

Atlantic Salmon Trust
Moulin
Pitlochry
Perthshire PH16 5JQ
Tel. 0796 3439

**British Association for Shooting and
Conservation**
Marford Mill
Chester Road
Rossett
Wrexham
Clwyd LL12 0HL
Tel. 0244 570881

British Deer Society
Church Farm
Lower Basildon
Reading, Berks. RG8 9NH
Tel. 073484 4094

British Falconers Club
J. R. Fairclough
Home Farm
Hints
Tamworth
Staffs. B78 3DW
Tel. 0543 481737

British Field Sports Society
59 Kennington Road
London SE1 7PZ
Tel. 071 928 4742
(Also **The Council for Country
Sports**)

Country Landowners Association
16 Belgrave Square
London SW1X 8PQ
Tel. 071 235 0511

English Nature
Northminster House
Peterborough PE1 1UA
Tel. 0733 340345

Forestry Commission
231 Corstorphine Road
Edinburgh EH12 7AT
Tel. 031 334 0303

The Game Conservancy
Fordingbridge
Hants. SP6 1EF
Tel. 0425 652381

Game Farmers Association
Major Barrington
Oddington Lodge
Moreton-in-the-Marsh
Glos.
Tel. 0451 30655

The Hawk Trust
C/O Birds of Prey Department
London Zoo
Regents Park
London NW1 4RY

**Masters of Basset Hounds
Association**
R. Schuster
The Grange
Nether Worton
Middle Barton
Oxon. OX5 4ES

Masters of Deer Hounds Association
Dr J. D. W. Peck
Bilboa House
Dulverton
Somerset TA22 9BW
   Tel. 0398 23475

Masters of Foxhounds Association
Parsloes Cottage
Bagendon
Cirencester
Glos.
   Tel. 028 583 470

National Birds of Prey Centre
Newent
Glos.
   Tel. 0531 820286

National Coursing Club
16 Clocktower Mews
Newmarket
Suffolk CB8 8LL
   Tel. 0638 667381

National Rivers Authority
Rivers House
30–34 Albert Embankment
London SE1 7TL
   Tel. 071 820 0101

Red Deer Commission
Knowlsry
82 Fairfield Road
Inverness IV3 5LH
   Tel. 04632 31751

**Royal Society for Nature
   Conservation**
The Green
Nettleham
Lincs. LN2 2NR
   Tel. 0522 544400

**Royal Society for the Protection of
   Birds**
The Lodge
Sandy
Beds.
   Tel. 0767 680551

Saint Hubert Club of Great Britain
A. Heathcoat
The Old Manor House
Hinxton
Saffron Waldon
Essex
   Tel. 0799 30496

Salmon and Trout Association
Fishmongers' Hall
London EC4
   Tel. 071 929 1389

Scottish Academy of Falconry
Mrs D. Durman-Walters
The Wigg
Borchester Bridge
Hawick TD9 9TB
   Tel. 045 086 666

**Standing Conference on Countryside
   Sports**
The College of Estate Management
Whiteknights
Reading
Berks RG6 2AW
   Tel. 0734 861101